Praise for *Messy People*
Life Lessons from Imperfect Biblical Heroes

Jennifer has a unique gift of making the Bible applicable to living a victorious life in everyday situations! This Bible study encourages, convicts, and equips us as we seek Jesus in all that we do.
— **Judy C. Graham**, President and Co-Founder, Celebration Women's Ministry, Inc.

If you've ever felt like your life is a mess, this study is for you. Jen is a down-to-earth, in-the-trenches, authentic follower of Christ who guides with humor and practical insights as to how we can allow God to turn our messes into His masterpieces. You will love the life application this study brings, freeing us up from the "chains" culture pushes us into.
— **Steve Gladen**, Pastor of Small Groups, Saddleback Church and author of
Leading Small Groups with Purpose

I have seen Jen's life and ministry up close and can say with confidence that her heart is for seeing messy lives get whole and healthy. Messy People is about finding hope, balance, peace, and wisdom by being immersed in the lessons of Scripture. Thanks, Jen, for pointing us back to the source of peace in the midst of a messy world.
— **Carolyn Moore**, Founding and Lead Pastor of Mosaic United Methodist Church
in Evans, Georgia, and author of *The 19: Questions to Kindle a
Wesleyan Spirit*

Using the Bible, humor, probing questions, and her own life experiences, Jennifer helps you break through the clutter and confusion of life to uncover your destiny and identity in Christ. You will discover the God who delights in making a masterpiece out of your mess.
— **Jorge Acevedo**, Lead Pastor of Grace Church, a multi-site United Methodist
congregation in Southwest Florida

By the power of story you will be escorted through the messy lives of biblical people, and in the process you'll discover something of yourself. Fueled by insightful commentary, real life experience, and "I get it" humor, you will be delightfully reminded that God "did, does, and will" use messy people.
— **Shane Bishop**, Senior Pastor of Christ Church in Fairview Heights, Illinois,
and recipient of The Foundation for Evangelism's Distinguished
Evangelist Award

Messy
PEOPLE

LIFE LESSONS *from* IMPERFECT
BIBLICAL HEROES

a Bible Study by

JENNIFER COWART

Abingdon Women
Nashville

Messy People
Life Lessons from Imperfect Biblical Heroes

ISBN 978-1-5018-6312-7

MANUFACTURED IN THE UNITED STATES OF AMERICA

(*Copyright page continues on page 205.*)

Contents

About the Author 6

Introduction 7

Week 1: Rahab: Changing Your Messy Story 10
(Joshua 2; 6)

Week 2: The Prodigal Son: Restoring Messy Relationships 38
(Luke 15:11-32)

Week 3: Josiah: Breaking Messy Family Cycles 68
(2 Kings 22–23; 2 Chronicles 34–35)

Week 4: Mary: Surviving Life's Messy Plot Twists 102
(Luke 1:26-38)

Week 5: David: Overcoming the Mess of Criticism 132
(1 Samuel 16–18; 2 Samuel 12; 15)

Week 6: Daniel: Thriving in Messy Circumstances 168
(Daniel 1–3)

Video Viewer Guide: Answers 202

Notes 203

About the Author

Jennifer Cowart is the Executive Pastor at Harvest Church, a United Methodist congregation in Warner Robins, Georgia, that she and her husband, Jim, began in 2001. Today, Harvest serves about 2,500 people in seven worship services weekly. With degrees in Christian education, counseling, and business, Jen oversees a wide variety of ministries and enjoys doing life and ministry with others. As a gifted Bible teacher and speaker, Jen brings biblical truth to life through humor, authenticity, and everyday application. She and Jim have co-written several small group studies together, including *Hand Me Downs* and *Living the Five*. They are the proud parents of two children, Alyssa and Josh.

Follow Jen:

 jimandjennifercowart

:fb: jimandjennifer.cowart

Website: jennifercowart.org or jimandjennifercowart.org

(check here for event dates and booking information)

Introduction

Hi, friend! Welcome to *Messy People*! Every life gets messy at times. Mine does, and surely yours does as well. Sometimes these messes are literal, like a house that would be easier to condemn than to clean or a child who needs a firehose instead of a tub. But sometimes our messes are harder to see. These intangible messes often have labels such as illness, conflict, depression, abuse, bankruptcy, divorce, and job loss. And often these messes are painful.

During this six-week study, we are going to dig into the lives of biblical heroes who were messy people too. Throughout the Scriptures we find wonderful but messy people God used in powerful ways. Together over these six weeks we will learn from the lives of Rahab, the prodigal son, Josiah, Mary, David, and Daniel. From their stories we will learn how God chooses to use broken people and how He restores damaged relationships. Through their examples we will see how God gives us power to handle our critics and deal with the hard moments of life.

This workbook contains six weeks' worth of devotional Bible lessons, with five lessons for each week. I call them devotional lessons because they include both Scripture study as well as reflection and prayer. I hope you'll give yourself the gift of time alone with God to savor His Word and allow Him to speak to you. You may want to find a quiet place—maybe your favorite chair or a spot on the porch, weather permitting—where you can spend your devotional study time.

Each day the lesson follows the same format:

Settle: As you begin each lesson, I encourage you to just be still for a few moments and allow your heart and mind to settle. In Psalm 46:10 we are told, "Be still, and know that I am God!" In the fast-paced world in which most of us operate, being still, breathing deeply, and resting in God's presence can be challenging. So, I encourage you as you begin each day's lesson to give yourself the sweet treasure of settling your heart, mind, and soul into your heavenly Father's presence. This alone can be a life-changer as you go through the study!

Focus: Next, focus your mind on God's Word, reading a thematic verse and a Scripture from the main story for the day. Isaiah 55:10-11 (TLB) has a promise for those who dwell on God's Word:

As the rain and snow come down from heaven and stay upon the ground to water the earth, and cause the grain to grow and to produce seed for the farmer and bread for the hungry, so also is my word. I send it out, and it always produces fruit. It shall accomplish all I want it to and prosper everywhere I send it.

Reflect: Now it's time to get to the story and think about how it speaks into your life. God's Word is so rich, and the stories of biblical heroes and heroines have so much to teach us. The lessons, triumphs, and tragedies of their lives are relevant to us today. As you consider these stories, which may be familiar to you, try to look at them with new eyes. Invite God to give you fresh insights to enrich your life. Space is provided for recording your responses and completing exercises.

Pray: Finally, be still once again and enter into a time of prayer, asking the Holy Spirit to speak new truths of peace and wisdom into your life. I will offer a few prayer suggestions each day to help your time with God be fresh and interesting.

As you begin and end each day's lesson, I encourage you to be creative in your approach to connecting with God. He is a creative genius; just look at the giraffe, butterfly, and anteater! Obviously, God likes variety and creativity. So at times I will encourage you to try some new things in the Settle and Prayer segments of the lessons. For instance, if you're musical, you may want to begin by singing or playing an instrument. If you're artistic, you may want to end each day by sketching or painting. Perhaps your gift is the written word; then journal what God is speaking to you. You also may want to incorporate praise and worship music (I have included a few song suggestions, but feel free to choose your own) as well as dance or stretching and other physical activity into your devotional study time. Be creative! Think outside your usual practices and try something new.

Before you get started, gather all the supplies you'll need: your Bible, this workbook, a pen or pencil, and any items you need for creative expression—such as a journal, a sketch pad, an instrument, or a device and playlist. Have your tools easily accessible so that nothing subtracts from your time. Another trick I've found helpful is to have a notepad handy so that if your thoughts begin to drift to things you need to do later, you can just jot them down so they do not steal your time with God.

As we begin this journey together, you may be going into, living in the midst of, or coming out of a messy moment; or you may have a loved one who is. If so, hang on—you're not alone. The Bible is filled with examples for us to follow of people who not only endured messy lives but actually thrived with God's guidance, and you can too. So get ready, because God is holding out His big, strong hands to you right in this moment and offering to take your messes and replace them with a masterpiece!

Enjoy your journey,

Jen

Week 1

Rahab

Changing Your Messy Story

Joshua 2; 6

DAY 1: GOD CHOOSES MESSY PEOPLE

Settle

Take a deep breath and release it slowly. You may want to do this a few times. As you breathe, allow the stresses of your day, the messes of the moment, to disappear. If only for these few minutes of your day, leave behind your struggles and give God your whole self.

Focus

But you are a chosen people, a royal priesthood, a holy nation, God's special possession.

(1 Peter 2:9 NIV)

Then Joshua secretly sent out two spies from the Israelite camp at Acacia Grove. He instructed them, "Scout out the land on the other side of the Jordan River, especially around Jericho." So the two men set out and came to the house of a prostitute named Rahab and stayed there that night.

(Joshua 2:1)

Read all of Rahab's story in Joshua 2 and 6.

Reflect

God chooses messy people!

I used to believe that if God needed something significant done, then He would choose someone who had it all together. Do you know those women? They have well-behaved children, dress beautifully, and never lose their cool. They plan their meals in advance and come to Bible study with the homework done and the key verse memorized. They order a salad at lunch and then pick off the croutons. If God wants to do something important, then that gal is the one for the job. Right?

Maybe. But then along comes a Bible hero like Rahab, and the perfect image is shattered. Rahab gives me hope that God can use messy people—maybe even me. In fact, her story teaches me that sometimes God chooses women with rough résumés and imperfect pasts to get His tough tasks done. Our heroine this week fits this description well. In fact, the idea that she is considered a heroine at all probably would have been a joke to those who knew her personally. You see, Rahab was a prostitute.

As we explore her story this week we will see how God chooses to use messy people. Isn't that amazing! The God of the universe chooses to use people with damaged reputations, broken hearts, and sinful pasts. That is good news for us. He knows us, redeems us, and longs to bring us into His family, just as He did for Rahab.

Think back to when you were a little girl. Who was your favorite princess: Snow White, Sleeping Beauty, the Little Mermaid, or another?

Mine was always Cinderella. Still is. I like the singing, sewing mice, "Bibbidi-Bobbidi-Boo," the carriage, the glass slipper—all of that stuff. But what I really love is that she was the princess who was chosen. Many of the other princesses of my childhood were great and beautiful, but they had been born into the right household; their parents were royalty. Cinderella, though, was ordinary. That I can relate to.

At the heart of most women is the deep desire to be chosen. As middle schoolers in the lunchroom, we worry that we won't be chosen to sit with the other kids. In high school we want to be chosen to go to prom. As adults we want to be chosen for the promotion, the team, the club—we just want to be chosen! Great news: you are! No matter how messy your life has been, no matter what you've done or how your story has unfolded so far—God loves you, and you are chosen. Rahab's story is a great example of how God chooses to love and use messy people.

When have you felt chosen in life? How did it make you feel?

So let's get to our Bible story. Rahab lives within the walls of the world's oldest continually inhabited city, Jericho.[1] She makes a living at the world's oldest occupation, prostitution. Jericho is the first city that Joshua comes to as God leads the Israelites across the Jordan River to conquer the land promised to the Israelites. The people who live in Jericho have heard of God and the miracles He has done for His people, but they worship pagan gods—not at all honoring the one true God.

Joshua, who has taken over leadership from his mentor, Moses, sends spies into Jericho on a reconnaissance mission. We read:

> Then Joshua secretly sent out two spies from the Israelite camp at Acacia Grove. He instructed them, "Scout out the land on the other side of the Jordan River, especially around Jericho." So the two men set out and came to the house of a prostitute named Rahab.
>
> (Joshua 2:1)

Now let's stop here for a moment. "A prostitute named Rahab." That's quite a title. Wouldn't you hate to live with a label like that? It would be like being known as "Sarah the liar" or "Rachel the drunk." Ouch! It would sting to be known by your worst quality.

What labels have you been given in life, and how have they affected you?

Have you ever felt disqualified from being used by God? Explain your response.

The men stay at Rahab's for the night. Not a bad place for men from out of town to blend in. But the king gets word that there may be spies in his kingdom, so he sends out soldiers to find them. Rahab agrees to cover for them in exchange for protection when the Israelites invade the city.

After the soldiers leave Rahab's home, she says to the Israelite spies:

> "I know the LORD has given you this land.... We are all afraid of you. Everyone in the land is living in terror. For we have heard how the LORD made a dry path for you through the Red Sea when you left Egypt.... For the LORD your God is the supreme God of the heavens above and the earth below.

"Now swear to me by the LORD that you will be kind to me and my family since I have helped you."

(Joshua 2:9-12a)

The spies agree, and when the Israelites conquer the city, Rahab and everyone in her household are spared (Joshua 6:22-23).

Was this a divine appointment that the spies would end up at Rahab's brothel? Maybe. Truthfully, we don't know. But we do know that God chose to use Rahab in a very difficult situation; she was an unlikely accomplice to God's plan.

This pagan woman, a prostitute living in a Canaanite town, recognizes and has faith in the God of Israel. She believes in a God she does not personally know but respects because of His amazing miracles. She even goes so far as to declare "the LORD your God is the supreme God of the heavens above and the earth below" (Joshua 2:11).

Read the verses below, and write your name in the blanks:

Even before he made the world, God loved _____ and chose _____ in Christ to be holy and without fault in his eyes.

(Ephesians 1:4)

You did not choose _____, but I chose _____ and appointed _____ so that _____ might go and bear fruit—fruit that will last—and so that whatever _____ ask[s] in my name the Father will give _____.

(John 15:16 NIV)

What do these Scriptures teach you about God's view of you?

Do you have a mirror handy? Take a look into it. (Really, go ahead and take a look!) Describe what you see:

When I look into the mirror, I see the flaws, the zits, the imperfections, and most recently, the wrinkles! But God doesn't. When God looks at each of us, He sees a masterpiece! Is it because the imperfections aren't really there? No, it's because He looks at things differently than we do.

Read 1 Samuel 16:7 in the margin. What does this verse tell us about how God sees us?

But the LORD said to Samuel, "Do not look on his appearance or on the height of his stature, because I have rejected him; for the LORD does not see as mortals see; they look on the outward appearance, but the LORD looks on the heart."
(1 Samuel 16:7 NRSV)

God looks beyond the flaws and sees who He created each of us to be. He sees someone He has chosen.

As a new mom, I looked at my tiny daughter, and all I saw was perfection. Still today, that's all I see. She may look in the mirror and want to lose a few pounds or wish she were taller or had longer hair, but I see who she was created to be. And she is beautiful! I see her potential and her beauty in ways that she may never be able to grasp. She is God's masterpiece. She is a gift in my life.

Are you able to look deeper than the outward appearance and see yourself as God does? Why or why not?

> **God looks beyond the flaws and sees who He created each of us to be. He sees someone He has chosen.**

What do you think God sees when He looks at you? Explain your response.

What does it mean for your life to know that God chooses you?

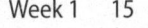

As you look in the mirror today, reflect on 1 Peter 2:9 (NIV): "You are a chosen people, a royal priesthood, a holy nation, God's special possession." God loves you! You are beautiful in His sight, and He wants to use you in great and wonderful ways!

Pray

- Take a deep breath and focus your thoughts on God.
- Thank God for seeing beyond your past and focusing on your potential.
- Take time to praise God for making you in His image—which is beautiful, by the way!
- Song suggestion: "Broken Things," recorded by Matthew West.

DAY 2: GOD USES MESSY PEOPLE

Settle

As you slow down, listen to Kari Jobe's recording of "Be Still My Soul" or another song of your choice, and allow the melody to calm you and center your heart on Christ.

Focus

For we are God's masterpiece. He has created us anew in Christ Jesus, so we can do the good things he planned for us long ago.

(Ephesians 2:10)

2But someone told the king of Jericho, "Some Israelites have come here tonight to spy out the land." 3So the king of Jericho sent orders to Rahab: "Bring out the men who have come into your house, for they have come here to spy out the whole land."

4Rahab had hidden the two men, but she replied, "Yes, the men were here earlier, but I didn't know where they were from. 5They left the town at dusk, as the gates were about to close. I don't know where they went. If you hurry, you can probably catch up with them." 6(Actually, she had taken them up to the roof and hidden them beneath bundles of flax she had laid out.) ...

8Before the spies went to sleep that night, Rahab went up on the roof to talk with them. 9"I know the LORD has given you this land," she told them. "We are all afraid of you. Everyone in the land is living in terror. 10For we have heard how the LORD made a dry path for you through the Red Sea when you left Egypt. 11 ...For the LORD your God is the supreme God of the heavens above and the earth below."

(Joshua 2:2-11)

Reflect

I grew up in church. I attended Sunday school, went on youth retreats, and dated Christian guys. By most people's standards I was a pretty good kid. So it's not surprising that my testimony is not that dramatic. In fact, it's a little boring. Now, I've come to appreciate boring, because it often leaves you with fewer messes; but again, it doesn't make for a very remarkable faith story.

But take someone like Rahab—now, there's a story! It reads like a major motion picture: a prostitute on the rough streets of Jericho who shelters spies and then engineers a daring escape. Later she is rescued along with her whole household when the city is attacked. Where is Emma Stone or Sandra Bullock? We need to make this film!

She is an unlikely heroine. Some may even wonder how God could use someone like Rahab, who had made so many mistakes and had such a messy past. But for me, I've often wondered the opposite. How could God use someone who has an ordinary story? As a teenager I had heard testimonies of how people far from God had dramatic conversion experiences and used their transformation to reach others who were like their former selves. If only I had a dramatic story too!

The truth is that messy people come in all shapes and sizes. Our churches are full of them, because when we get right down to it, messy people are simply people with sin in their lives.

Read Romans 3:23 in the margin. Who are the messy people who sin?

For everyone has sinned; we all fall short of God's glorious standard.
(Romans 3:23)

Sin is a condition that affects us all, yet God chooses each of us and wants to use us if we will let Him. God uses sinners. Of course God uses sinners; it's all He's got to work with, right?

Reread Ephesians 2:10 (page 17). According to this verse, why does God make us new creations in Jesus?

This verse teaches us that we have been created to be used by God to do amazing things, and Jesus makes this possible! It tells us that, in Christ, we are masterpieces in God's eyes, and He wants to use everyone for His purposes.

We know this at one level; but when He chooses to use someone with a notorious past, it usually gets our attention. The spies didn't show up on the doorstep of a priest or a "good person" in Jericho. They chose a brothel. They ended up at the home of Rahab, a sinner. But she was much more than that. She was clever and worldly, and she handled stress well. Under pressure, she had the presence of mind to keep cool and devise a way to save not only the spies but also her entire family in the process. The lessons that a hard-lived life had taught her were not wasted when God called upon her to help His people. God uses messy people. God also uses those who respond in faith.

When and how have you noticed that God often uses unlikely people to accomplish His will?

We have been created to be used by God to do amazing things, and Jesus makes this possible!

Consider the disciples. Peter, James, John, and Andrew were fishermen. They were tough and calloused men who worked demanding jobs. Not being candidates for priestly training, they probably had received little formal education and, instead, had taken to the family business of fishing. When Jesus called them, everything changed. They were no longer rejected; they were chosen. Matthew, another disciple, was a tax collector. He was perhaps educated but surely not well liked as a tax official in the Galilean region. These are some of the men Jesus personally chose as His closest companions. Their lives are recorded for us to see thousands of years later, but how were they qualified?

Let's look at a few of their stories and see what stands out.

Read the following verses and underline the descriptions of how the disciples responded to Jesus.

[18]One day as Jesus was walking along the shore of the Sea of Galilee, he saw two brothers—Simon, also called Peter, and Andrew—throwing a net into the water, for they fished for a living. [19]Jesus called out to them, "Come, follow me, and I will show you how to fish for people!" [20]And they left their nets at once and followed him.

[21]A little farther up the shore he saw two other brothers, James and John, sitting in a boat with their father, Zebedee, repairing their

nets. And he called them to come, too. ²²They immediately followed him, leaving the boat and their father behind.

(Matthew 4:18-22)

As Jesus went on from there, he saw a man named Matthew sitting at the tax collector's booth. "Follow me," he told him, and Matthew got up and followed him.

(Matthew 9:9 NIV)

What does this reveal to us about their one qualification?

We don't see any perfect pedigrees here. There are no qualifications that seem to set them apart from others. What we see are messy people with a willingness to respond to the call of God. They were willing to alter their plans for God. In fact, the words at once and immediately almost jump off the page. These men responded *at once, immediately*, in faith! Just like Rahab.

When God taps you on the heart, how quickly do you tend to respond?

When you consider how God might want to use you, what obstacles do you feel are holding you back?

How do you feel when you think of God using Rahab the prostitute?

How do you feel when you think of God using *you*?

Now, let's get back to our heroine, Rahab. When presented with the opportunity to help God's people, she is quick to respond in spite of her fears. In fact, she says her people are not only afraid but are living in terror. When you have the opportunity to serve God, there will be times when it is simple and sweet; but at other times, it will be terrifying. It will be messy, scary, and uncertain. That, my friend, is when the opportunity for faith comes, and that is when heroines emerge.

Pray

- Consider your faith story, and thank God for how He has shown up despite your imperfections.
- Focus on what God would have you move past in order to live your best life now.
- Ask God to help you be ready to respond immediately as He calls your name this week.

DAY 3: GOD SEES MESSY PEOPLE

Settle

Set a timer for two minutes, and just be still. That's it: just be quiet and let the troubles of today fall away for at least two minutes, enjoying the quiet of the moment.

Focus

"You shall love your neighbor as yourself." There is no other commandment greater . . .

(Mark 12:31 NKJV)

[12]*"Now swear to me by the LORD that you will be kind to me and my family since I have helped you. Give me some guarantee that* [13]*when Jericho is conquered, you will let me live." . . .*

[14]*"We offer our own lives as a guarantee for your safety," the men agreed.*

(Joshua 2:12-14)

Reflect

My husband, Jim, and I have two children, Alyssa and Josh—two amazing, wonderful, completely different kids. When they were little, Alyssa was shy. She would hide her face in my knees when we went into new settings. Josh, on the other hand, would go to the play area at a fast-food restaurant, stand on the slide, and yell, "Hey, I'm Josh! Who wants to be my friend?" He never met a stranger, which is kind of scary for a mom of a toddler.

To this day, he surprises me at his boldness in some situations. Recently while shopping, Josh waited outside the store for me. (Don't panic. He's a seventeen-year-old weight lifter. All is well!) He came and found me after about twenty minutes and said, "Hey, Mom, meet Melvin. I told him we'd fix him up with a few things." My first question: "Fix him up with what?" Second question: "Who in the world is Melvin?"

Turns out that Josh had seen a homeless man and approached him to find out his story and see what he needed. Melvin was messy. He was sick and hadn't bathed in quite a while. Truthfully, he was a tough-looking guy. We were able to help him out a little bit, and a sweet friendship developed.

But as I have reflected on the initial scenario, I have wondered what gave Josh the courage to approach this guy and ask him about his life.

Would I have done that?

I, and so many others like me that day, had not really noticed Melvin. We had walked by without seeing him. But Josh saw him, really saw him. He took the time to get to know Melvin and learn his story.

Reread Mark 12:31 (page 22). What did Jesus command us to do? Why do you think there is no greater commandment?

This verse makes me think of Rahab. If I had been a resident of Jericho, would I have associated with Rahab? Would I have asked her about her life? Would we have been friends? Maybe, but probably not. Surely we would have hung out with different crowds. I mean, she would have been a messy person, right?

But here's the problem. I'm messy too. I am just a different kind of messy.

Have you ever had a time when you wanted someone to *really* see you—to notice the pain you're in and offer to intervene? If so, briefly describe that time.

What kinds of messy people make you uncomfortable? How do you respond to them?

Rahab is not the only noteworthy resident of Jericho. More than one thousand years after Rahab saved the Israelite spies, Jesus visits this same town and encounters another messy person.

¹*Jesus entered Jericho and was passing through. ²A man was there by the name of Zacchaeus; he was a chief tax collector and was wealthy. ³He wanted to see who*

Jesus was, but because he was short he could not see over the crowd. ⁴So he ran ahead and climbed a sycamore-fig tree to see him, since Jesus was coming that way.

⁵When Jesus reached the spot, he looked up and said to him, "Zacchaeus, come down immediately. I must stay at your house today." ⁶So he came down at once and welcomed him gladly.

⁷All the people saw this and began to mutter, "He has gone to be the guest of a sinner."

(Luke 19:1-7 NIV)

The crowds have assembled as Jesus enters town. At this point in His ministry, wherever He goes, the crowds come. His teachings and healings are well known by the time we get to the nineteenth chapter of Luke's Gospel. The crowd is so thick that Zacchaeus can't get a glimpse of Jesus, so he climbs a tree.

As the teacher passes by, He sees Zacchaeus. This shocks the crowd because Zacchaeus is not a popular guy. (Tax collectors of this time were notorious for overtaxing and cheating people.) When Jesus looks up, calls this man by name, and then goes to his home, the crowd is not pleased. Why would Jesus choose Zacchaeus?

What must Zacchaeus be thinking? Surely he hears the crowd as they begin to mutter against him. But he also hears Jesus as He calls him by name!

This "wee little man," as the children's song describes him, has been small in stature and short on respect his whole life. But as Jesus looks at him, He calls Zacchaeus by name. He is saying, "I see you, Zacchaeus. I know you, and I care about you. Come on down, and let's spend time together."

Jesus knows your name too! He sees you. Don't miss that. Jesus knows you. He knows your name—and what you weigh, no matter what your driver's license says! He knows about the dust bunnies under the stove and the bills you owe. And He cares.

In Africa, "I see you" is an ancient greeting. It is simple but also deep—more than a statement of being able to visually comprehend someone's presence. It is a sign that I acknowledge you—I see your worth and give you honor. While visiting in Uganda last year, I had a Maasai tribesman approach me and give this greeting after a few days together: "I see you, Jennifer." It was a warm greeting of honor.

Jesus looks at you fresh each day and whispers, "I see you."

As you consider that Jesus truly sees you and all that you are dealing with today, how does that make you feel?

God calls us to love messy people.

Is there someone you need to slow down and notice today? Whom might it be?

What can you offer to help this person feel valued?

How can you help to meet her or his needs?

Let's go back to Josh and Melvin. When Josh came into the store to find me, he brought Melvin with him. This caused a bit of a commotion. In fact, the commotion is what first got my attention.

As I heard the store clerk telling Melvin that he needed to leave, Josh touched the clerk's hand and said, "No, ma'am, he's with me." It was the Great Commandment in action: "Love one another" (John 13:34 NIV). God calls us to love messy people.

Who has taken the time to really see you?

God sees you, but He also sees those around you. Once you discover God's love personally, He wants you to share that with others. We are to love even the messy people living in the tough parts of town, or that family member who has gone astray, or the friend who is making poor choices. These people are Zacchaeus. They are Rahab. And, at times, they are you and me.

Pray

- For an energized time of prayer, listen and even dance along with Hollyn's recording of "Love with Your Life." (I bet you'll move at least a little bit as you listen!)
- Thank God for seeing you and caring about every detail of your life.
- Ask God who He would have you reach out to in love today. Then do it!

DAY 4: GOD REDEEMS
MESSY PEOPLE

Settle

As you quiet your heart today, sing or hum a simple song that brings you peace—perhaps one you learned as a child or new Christian. It could be something as simple as "Jesus Loves Me" or "Amazing Grace." For me, a song that brings peace is Sandi Patty's "O Calvary's Lamb." I sang it over my children's cribs to put them to sleep. Whatever you choose, allow that familiar, simple tune to center your thoughts on God.

Focus

Therefore, if anyone is in Christ, the new creation has come: The old has gone, the new is here!

(2 Corinthians 5:17 NIV)

15Then, since Rahab's house was built into the town wall, she let them down by a rope through the window. 16"Escape to the hill country," she told them. . . .

17Before they left, the men told her, "We will be bound by the oath we have taken only if you follow these instructions. 18When we come into the land, you must leave this scarlet rope hanging from the window through which you let us down. And all your family members—your father, mother, brothers, and all your relatives—must be here inside the house. 19If they go out into the street and are killed, it will not be our fault. But if anyone lays a hand on people inside this house, we will accept the responsibility for their death. 20If you betray us, however, we are not bound by this oath in any way."

21"I accept your terms," she replied. And she sent them on their way, leaving the scarlet rope hanging from the window.

(Joshua 2:15-21)

Reflect

When my kids were little, keeping the house clean was an ongoing battle. In fact, the only time I really cleaned and straightened was when my husband took the kids and left for a while. I would go into speed mode, picking up toys, cleaning, vacuuming, doing laundry; and then, every time, it happened. They returned. And with them came the mess—the mess of crumbs and toys and diapers and spit-up. The mess was back.

I came to love a peculiar verse during that stage of life: "An empty stable stays clean—but there is no income from an empty stable" (Proverbs 14:4 TLB). This verse took on so many meanings for me.

First, a house without children certainly is easier to keep clean, but what a joy to experience that messy time of life with my crusty kiddos. I can still remember the pungent odor that assaulted me when opening a car door with a three-day-old sippy cup inside. And I remember the frustration of spending an hour getting dressed up for my first time out of the house in a week only to have one of the kids throw up on me as I walked out the door. Where the stable is clean, it is also empty.

Second, I began to look at this verse through the lens of ministry. When a church is full, it's messy. Once people get involved, there will be messes. That's a guarantee. And those messes are much worse than spit-up and half-eaten crackers. They leave scars. Instead of requiring buckets of bleach, these messes require massive amounts of faith and forgiveness. But messy people are who Jesus came for, and it's our privilege as Christ-followers to do life with one another.

You and I are messy people. So was Rahab.

Mess in the sense of scattered toys and spilled milk is one thing, but the kind of messes we are dealing with in this study are more accurately called sin. Rahab was caught in the mess of prostitution, a public sexual sin. Sometimes the messes we are caught in are apparent, just as Rahab's sin was, but sometimes they are more subtle—easier to cover up and disguise. Yet that in no way lessens the damage that sin does in the lives of those who are trapped, as well as the lives of those who love them.

I spend a great deal of my week talking with people who are hurting because of sin. After years in ministry, it still saddens me to hear about the secret sins that are destroying families. Affairs, pornography, abuse, addictions, lies, and gambling are a few examples of sins that are wreaking havoc not only in our society but also in our churches. On a less dramatic but equally devastating level, there are sins such as selfishness, gossip, and mean-spirited interactions that are drawing people, including Christians, away from what God would have for their lives.

I've realized that in order for me to really love people deeply and help them work through the messes of their lives, I must first work on the messes in my life. On an airplane we are instructed to put on the oxygen mask first before trying to help someone else. If we're not breathing, we won't be able to help anyone else. So, before becoming concerned with others' sins, we must take a look at our own.

The first step in cleaning up our lives is to acknowledge our own sins.

Read 1 John 1:8 in the margin. What does this in-your-face verse say we're doing if we claim to be without sin?

If we claim to be without sin, we deceive ourselves and the truth is not in us.

(1 John 1:8 NIV)

Being able to move forward in faith involves acknowledging our sin, repenting, and living in a way that honors God. So get honest with yourself right now—really honest. You may not even have the courage to write it down, but at least think about this next question seriously.

What messes are you caught in right now?

> **Before becoming concerned with others' sins, we must take a look at our own.**

Rahab shelters the spies, but her story does not end there.

Read Joshua 6:22-25. What happens to Rahab and her family?

What reason is given in verse 25?

At the end of Joshua 6, Rahab and her entire household are rescued. Because of her bold faithfulness, she and her family are redeemed. God has seen her faith, chosen her, used her, and redeemed her. Now her story is changed forever. She overcomes the sins of her past and is used in new and powerful ways.

God wants to do the same for you! "Therefore, if anyone is in Christ, the new creation has come: The old has gone, the new is here!" (2 Corinthians 5:17 NIV).

How might God be wanting to change your story the way He changed Rahab's?

What steps of faith do you need to take for that to happen?

Who in your life may need your help to change their story?

You and I are messy people, and so are the people in our lives. Just as our own messes can paralyze us, sometimes the messes in the lives of others can seem so overwhelming that we simply want to walk away. But let's not do that. As we see in Rahab's story, God's spies needed her in order to escape, but she needed them too. The same is true of us. We need one another.

Pray

- Just be still.
- Thank God for turning your messes into a masterpiece—even if you can't see it yet.
- Seek God's forgiveness for the sins that have made a mess of your life.
- Ask God how you might partner with someone who is trapped in a mess.
- Song suggestion: "Chain Breaker," recorded by Zach Williams.

DAY 5: GOD GIVES MESSY PEOPLE A ROYAL LINEAGE

Settle

If you play an instrument, begin today by playing to the Lord. If you're artistic, draw a sketch of some part of God's creation that brings you peace. If neither applies to you, just take out pencil and paper and list the things of God's creation that bring you peace and joy.

Focus

God decided in advance to adopt us into his own family by bringing us to himself through Jesus Christ. This is what he wanted to do, and it gave him great pleasure.

(Ephesians 1:5)

22Joshua said to the two spies, "Keep your promise. Go to the prostitute's house and bring her out, along with all her family."

23The men who had been spies went in and brought out Rahab, her father, mother, brothers, and all the other relatives who were with her. They moved her whole family to a safe place near the camp of Israel.

24Then the Israelites burned the town and everything in it. Only the things made from silver, gold, bronze, or iron were kept for the treasury of the LORD's house. 25So Joshua spared Rahab the prostitute and her relatives who were with her in the house, because she had hidden the spies Joshua sent to Jericho. And she lives among the Israelites to this day.

(Joshua 6:22-25)

Reflect

Recently my husband was asked about his ancestry, to which he replied, "Um, I'm just regular, I guess." We all chuckled at that, but as his greatest admirer, I thought, *No, you're not regular.* You're awesome! What nationality does awesome come from?

No matter what kind of family you are born into...you have the option to be adopted into a royal lineage....You have the choice to be in Jesus' family!

As I thought about that conversation later, I wondered why it troubled me to hear him say, "I'm regular." It was because I know different—not that I know he is Italian or Scottish, but that I know he is part of a royal family. He has been adopted into a kingly family!

Read the following verses, underlining the words that describe our identity in Christ:

You are a chosen people, a royal priesthood, a holy nation, God's special possession, that you may declare the praises of him who called you out of darkness into his wonderful light.

(1 Peter 2:9 NIV)

God decided in advance to adopt us into his own family by bringing us to himself through Jesus Christ. This is what he wanted to do, and it gave him great pleasure.

(Ephesians 1:5)

So in Christ Jesus you are all children of God through faith.

(Galatians 3:26 NIV)

I love that! No matter what kind of family you are born into—wealthy or poor, healthy or dysfunctional—you have the option to be adopted into a royal lineage. You can be a daughter—no, a princess—to the King of kings. You have the choice to be in Jesus' family! And that is not just "regular"!

But how does it happen? How do we move from ordinary citizen to a member of the royal household? It's all through faith. By placing our faith in Christ, God becomes our Father, we become His children, other believers become our brothers and sisters, and the church becomes our spiritual family.

God's unchanging plan always has been "to adopt us into his own family by bringing us to himself through Jesus Christ. This is what he wanted to do, and it gave him *great pleasure*" (Ephesians 1:5, emphasis added).

Read Matthew 12:49-50 in the margin. What does Jesus say about those who follow Him?

49Then he pointed to his disciples and said, "Look, these are my mother and brothers. 50Anyone who does the will of my Father in heaven is my brother and sister and mother!"
(Matthew 12:49-50)

We have all been created in the image of God, but to become His child—a princess—requires a response. The invitation to be part of God's family is universal, but there is one condition: faith in Jesus. This is our RSVP to God's invitation. Faith is what makes adoption into God's family possible. By accepting Jesus as Lord of our lives and seeking forgiveness of our sins, we move from creation of God to child of the King!

This week we have looked at an unlikely heroine, Rahab. She shelters the spies, and in turn she and her whole family are saved when the Israelites invade Jericho.

Look again at Joshua 6:25. How is Rahab named or described here?

She's rescued, but there's that label again: Rahab the prostitute. We would think she was just a messy woman who helped God's people out once upon a time if we didn't see her mentioned again in a very unexpected place.

Read Matthew 1:5-6 (NIV) and fill in the blanks below:

Salmon was the father of Boaz, whose mother was_____,

Boaz was the father of Obed, whose mother was Ruth,

Obed was the father of Jesse,

and Jesse the father of _____ _____.

Here at the beginning of the New Testament in the first chapter of Matthew, we have a family tree—Jesus' family tree. And it's in this distinguished lineage that Rahab appears. She is King David's great-great-grandmother. This is a family tree that eventually leads us to Jesus Himself! How does this happen? How does Rahab the prostitute turn into Rahab the great-great-grandmother of the great King David?

For that matter, how does anyone caught in a difficult life situation move from messy to masterpiece?

I have a dear friend who had a difficult upbringing—not much money, not much consistency from the adults in her life. It's not a great story, honestly. That is, not until she decided to change the outcome of her story. She simply made a choice to lovingly distance herself from the unhealthy things of her past and seek new patterns. This was a tough decision, and for years she did it through sheer willpower. Then she met Jesus. Through His power in her life and the guidance of the Holy Spirit, she has turned what could have been a tragic outcome into a beautiful life of serving Christ and others.

My friend, like Rahab, changed her story through faith and obedience to God.

When Rahab first encounters the Israelite spies, she expresses faith in the power of their God. But when she moves into action for their God, He becomes her God. We don't know the details of what happens after Rahab is rescued in Jericho, but we do know that she becomes part of the Hebrew community. She marries and raises a family. She is changed. And as we've seen, the very lineage of Jesus is impacted through the faithfulness of this messy woman.

At what point did God become your God?

In the same way, was not even Rahab the prostitute considered righteous for what she did when she gave lodging to the spies and sent them off in a different direction?

(James 2:25 NIV)

We see Rahab yet again in Scripture. She is mentioned in the books of James and Hebrews.

Look up Hebrews 11, noting the many heroes commended for their faith in this chapter. Write some of their names below:

According to verse 31, what saved Rahab?

Now read James 2:25 in the margin. How was Rahab viewed after she helped the spies?

Hebrews 11 is known as the Hall of Faith chapter. In this passage the writer lists some of the very greatest heroes of Scripture such as Abel, Abraham, Jacob, Joseph, and Moses. And mentioned by name in this prestigious company is our heroine, Rahab! If you're going to be mentioned anywhere in the Bible, this is a great place to be! But consider the messy lives and the excuses these heroes could have hidden behind:

- Abraham was elderly.
- Joseph was mistreated.
- Moses was a stutterer.
- Gideon was penniless.
- David was an adulterer.
- Jonah was a coward.
- Naomi was a widow.
- Peter was a hothead.
- Rahab was immoral.

What a group! Yet through their faith, God was able to use them in mighty ways! Like Rahab, they all changed their stories. They did not let their failures define them. Though their lives were messy, just like ours, they moved past their old reputations into their roles in God's family.

God has a place in His family for you too. As we close this week, I hope that you will choose either to join or renew your commitment to God's family. Remember, God chooses to use messy people like me and you!

Pray

- If you have not received Jesus as your Savior, pray for forgiveness of your sins and ask God to be the center of your life—the author of your story!
- If you already are a Christ-follower, take time to recommit yourself to Jesus today.
- Thank God for adopting you into His royal family.
- Song suggestion: "Good Good Father," recorded by Chris Tomlin.

VIDEO VIEWER GUIDE: WEEK 1

Then Joshua secretly sent out two spies from the Israelite camp at Acacia Grove.

(Joshua 2:1)

"I know the LORD has given you this land . . . we have heard how the LORD made a dry path for you through the Red Sea when you left Egypt."

(Joshua 2:9-10)

And Joshua saved Rahab the harlot alive, and her father's household, and all that she had; and she dwelleth in Israel even unto this day; because she hid the messengers, which Joshua sent to spy out Jericho.

(Joshua 6:25 KJV)

Simple (but not always easy) steps for moving from mess to best:

1. Recognize our _____need_____ for God.

You will seek the LORD your God . . . and you will find him if you seek him with all your heart and with all your being.

(Deuteronomy 4:29 CEB)

2. Resolve to lead a life that is _____centered_____ in Christ.

Decide in advance

Don't be conformed to the patterns of this world, but be transformed by the renewing of your minds so that you can figure out what God's will is—what is good and pleasing and mature.

(Romans 12:2 CEB)

3. Request help from ___*Godly people*___.

Without guidance, a people will fall,

    but there is victory with many counselors.

              (Proverbs 11:14 CEB)

4. Remember Who holds your ___*future*___.

"For I know the plans that I have for you," declares the Lord, *"plans for welfare and not for calamity to give you a future and a hope."*

                  (Jeremiah 29:11 NASB)

Week 2

The Prodigal Son

Restoring Messy Relationships

Luke 15:11-32

DAY 1: COME TO YOUR SENSES

Settle

Stand up and take a deep breath in, reaching over your head as you hold that breath a few seconds, and then slowly exhale. Now try it again. Invite the Holy Spirit in with each breath; and as you breathe out, release the stresses that would distract you as you spend time with Jesus today.

Focus

Come back to your senses as you ought, and stop sinning.
(1 Corinthians 15:34 NIV)

[11]"A man had two sons. [12]The younger son told his father, 'I want my share of your estate now before you die.' So his father agreed to divide his wealth between his sons.

[13]"A few days later this younger son packed all his belongings and moved to a distant land, and there he wasted all his money in wild living. [14]About the time his money ran out, a great famine swept over the land, and he began to starve. [15]He persuaded a local farmer to hire him, and the man sent him into his fields to feed the pigs. [16]The young man became so hungry that even the pods he was feeding the pigs looked good to him. But no one gave him anything.

[17]"When he finally came to his senses, he said to himself, 'At home even the hired servants have food enough to spare, and here I am dying of hunger! [18]I will go home to my father and say, "Father, I have sinned against both heaven and you, [19]and I am no longer worthy of being called your son. Please take me on as a hired servant."' "

(Luke 15:11-19)

Also read Luke 15:1-10.

Reflect

What keeps you up at night?

For many the answer to this question is worry. Worry about finances, the kids, a friend, the job, what needs to get done tomorrow, the future—the list can seem endless. Years ago I decided that whenever worry crept into my brain, I would crush it like a bug with prayer. And it has worked, except for one area.

So let me confess something to you: what keeps me up at night is worrying about broken relationships. With God's help through prayer, I can deal with people who are having a crisis, battling cancer, or grieving the loss of a loved one—and even deal with my own grief and sadness. But if I am involved in a messy relationship, it literally wakes me up at night.

I do all of the mental gymnastics of "what if" and "if only." If only I had said this. What if I call in the morning? If only they understood. What if they were in my shoes? It's not productive, and I don't suggest it. But that's my struggle. Simply stated, I hate broken relationships! Yet as members of the human race, they are inevitable.

This week we will explore how to respond when we have a messy relationship. And we'll do it by digging into a familiar story that most people know as the parable of the prodigal son. Personally, I prefer to think of it as the parable of two lost sons or, even better, as the parable of the father who ran.

In the fifteenth chapter of the Gospel of Luke, we read several stories about lost things: a lost sheep, a lost coin, and a lost boy. There is great emphasis on what is lost because God cares about what is lost. In fact, it's what Christmas and Easter are all about. Redeeming lost people is why God sent Jesus: "For the Son of Man came to seek and to save the lost" (Luke 19:10 NIV).

Here's a summary of the story. A wealthy man has two sons. His younger son very rudely informs his father that he doesn't want to wait until the father dies to receive his share of the inheritance. The father gives his son his wish and gives him his share immediately. The son then moves away and wastes his money on "wild living" (Luke 15:13). (You can imagine what may have been involved in that scenario.) When his money runs out, so do his friends. Becoming hungry, he takes a job feeding pigs—not something a proper Jewish man would want to do. He even begins to consider eating the pig's slop! So in desperation, the son swallows his pride and goes home, hoping to be taken in as a hired servant. But his father does not receive him as a servant. Instead, he welcomes him with love and throws him a party!

Now, let's dig into this story. Can you imagine how this dad feels when his son comes to him demanding his portion of inheritance? Not only is it rude to say, "I don't want to wait until you die to get my money," but then the father watches his son leave home, knowing that most likely he will not make good decisions with these funds. There is a break in this relationship. There is a break geographically and, more important, emotionally. As a result, this father likely will spend many restless nights being concerned and hurting for his son.

What broken relationships have kept you up at night?

Have you ever experienced a break in a relationship within your family? How did it make you feel?

In Luke 15:17 we read, "When he finally came to his senses, [the son] said to himself, 'At home even the hired servants have food enough to spare, and here I am dying of hunger!'"

"When he finally came to his senses...." I like that description. Here is this young man who has completely severed his relationship with family. He has squandered his inheritance and is now destitute, literally starving, while at home even the servants have enough.

Surely before he got to this low point he could have examined his life and realized he was in trouble. But he didn't. It took extreme pain before he examined his life, sought wisdom, and took steps to improve his situation. Sometimes it takes a low point for us to come to our senses too.

When you face a difficult circumstance, what do you do?

Specifically, when that circumstance is a broken relationship, how do you handle it?

Perhaps, like me, you lay awake at night and worry—again, not productive. So instead, let me share a few ideas that are helpful.

> Sometimes it takes a low point for us to come to our senses.

First, seek God's help. Matthew 7:7 tells us, "Ask and it will be given to you; seek and you will find; knock and the door will be opened to you" (NIV). If you get serious about restoring a damaged relationship, you're going to need God's help. So go there first.

Second, seek wisdom. This means looking at things from God's perspective instead of from your own. James 1:5 says, "If any of you lacks wisdom, you should ask God, who gives generously to all without finding fault, and it will be given to you" (NIV). Moving beyond your own understanding to gain God's perspective will give you new insights.

Third, seek to understand rather than to be understood. Philippians 2:4 instructs us, "Let each of you look not only to his own interests, but also to the interests of others" (ESV). This verse will change your life if you begin to live it out. Taking the time and emotional energy to really understand others' feelings, hurts, and desires is a key to unlocking healthy and mature relationships. Intentionally becoming considerate of others will, in itself, bring a great deal of healing.

All have sinned and fall short of the glory of God.
(Romans 3:23 NIV)

Read Romans 3:23 in the margin. Who is exempt from sin?

No one is exempt from sin. Recognizing our own sin is the first step in repairing broken relationships. So when the prodigal son comes to his senses, recognizing his own sin, it is the beginning of restoration.

What do you need to recognize and admit in order to bring healing to some of the brokenness in your life?

How can you begin a peacemaking process with someone this week?

First Peter 4:8 (NIV) says, "Above all, love each other deeply, because love covers over a multitude of sins." This is one of those verses that I hear in my head repeatedly when I'm aggravated with someone, hurt, disappointed, or angry. It plays again and again in my brain—"Above all, love each other deeply." When I hear this I think, "Okay, Jen, come to your senses. Get over yourself. Go make things right to the best of your ability." Coming to our senses and choosing to love others deeply are the first steps in restoring our broken relationships.

Pray

- Take time to write a letter to God as your prayer today, asking God to lead you in restoring a broken relationship this week.
- Listen to "What Faith Can Do," recorded by Kutless, or another song of your choice about faith.

Coming to our senses and choosing to love others deeply are the first steps in restoring our broken relationships.

DAY 2: TAKE RESPONSIBILITY

Settle

Take time as you begin to listen to "Never Been a Moment," recorded by Micah Tyler, and reflect on God's steadfast love for you. Or choose another song, or a Scripture passage, that speaks of God's faithful love.

Focus

For we are each responsible for our own conduct.
(*Galatians 6:5*)

[18]*"I will go home to my father and say, 'Father, I have sinned against both heaven and you,* [19]*and I am no longer worthy of being called your son. Please take me on as a hired servant.'"*

(*Luke 15:18-19*)

Reflect

Taking responsibility for our mistakes brings healing into messy relationships.

My husband loves horses and often spends his days at a farm riding on some beautiful wooded trails. In his adventures, time sometimes gets away from him and he comes home later than expected. We've been late to dinner gatherings and missed our movie night numerous times when this happens. And sometimes it really aggravates me. Over the years he has learned not to explain where he was and what happened. Instead, his first words when he walks in the door are, "I'm sorry; I was wrong." It actually sucks the wind out of whatever I had been getting ready to say. It's a great strategy for making peace.

When he steps up and owns the fact that he was inconsiderate, it places the ball in my court. Do I stay mad or forgive him? Honestly, if it happened all the time, I wouldn't think his apology was sincere, but it doesn't. It's a once-in-a-while thing; and I know that in the joy of riding, he just loses track of time. So could I stay mad? Sure. Would that be productive? No.

Taking responsibility for our mistakes brings healing into messy relationships.

Yesterday we took a look at the first part of the famous parable of the prodigal son in Luke 15. Our emphasis was on coming to our senses and seeking God's help for insight and wisdom. That is a first step to resolving conflict and moving forward.

As we read yesterday, the prodigal son comes to his senses in verse 17, becoming aware that he has made a mistake: "When he finally came to his senses, [the son] said to himself, 'At home even the hired servants have food enough to spare, and here I am dying of hunger! I will go home to my father and say, "Father, I have sinned against both heaven and you."'" (Luke 15:17-18). But will he have the humility to take responsibility for it? Will he go home and seek reconciliation?

The next verses are critical to the outcome of this parable.

Reread Luke 15:18-19 on page 44. What does the son resolve to do? What does he plan to say to his father?

The prodigal takes responsibility for his sin against both his earthly father and his heavenly one. He is prepared to apologize and take the consequences for his behavior. The younger son not only acknowledges his responsibility but also determines to do his best to move toward reconciliation.

Now, in this particular parable it is easy to see where the blame lies. It is with the prodigal. But in real life, fault usually lies on both sides of a broken relationship. Often instead of both parties working together to fix the relationship, we fix the blame. That's not what the prodigal does. We don't see him whine or blame his family or his wild-living friends. Rather, he humbles himself and owns his sin.

Taking responsibility is key to the restoration we see in this story.

Galatians 6:5 teaches us that "we are each responsible for our own conduct." In order to build strong, healthy relationships, we must be willing to step up and be responsible for those times when we blow it. But in order to do that, we have to overcome a nasty obstacle: pride.

Do you have a problem with pride? Most of us would say no. But the answer may be different if we dig a little deeper and ask questions such as these:

- Have you ever taken credit when it should have been shared with someone else?
- Do you find it hard to back down once you've said something, even when you know you may not be correct?

- Have you ever put someone down in a way that made yourself look good?
- Have you ever refused to say "I'm sorry" because you didn't want to look weak?
- Do you become defensive when you realize you've made a mistake?

Answering yes to any of these questions is a symptom of pride. Pride often prevents us from admitting when we are wrong. It's selfish pride that keeps us from saying "I'm sorry," and it is the source of many broken relationships.

Can you identify a time when your pride caused damage to a relationship? If so, describe it briefly:

22But the Holy Spirit produces this kind of fruit in our lives: love, joy, peace, patience, kindness, goodness, faithfulness, 23gentleness, and self-control. There is no law against these things!
(Galatians 5:22-23)

When we look up the definition of pride, we see a list of synonyms such as arrogance, self-love, conceit, and vanity. These qualities are in opposition to a woman who is seeking to honor God in her life. Instead, we should want to see in our lives what is known as the fruit of the Spirit.

Read Galatians 5:22-23 in the margin. What produces this fruit in our lives?

When conflict arises in your relationships, instead of responding with a defensive attitude or seeking to get your own way, strive to respond with the fruit of the Spirit: love, joy, peace, patience, kindness, goodness, faithfulness, gentleness, and self-control. This is a mature response.

Circle the aspects of the fruit of the Spirit that you want to focus on this week:

Love	**Joy**	**Peace**
Patience	**Kindness**	**Goodness**
Faithfulness	**Gentleness**	**Self-Control**

What can you do to cooperate with the Holy Spirit in order to increase this fruit in your life?

Think for a moment about immaturity. Take babies, for instance. They cry when wet and demand care when hungry. Babies require constant attention. Or consider a newly planted tree. It needs water and fertilizer and protection from storms in its immature years. In early stages of growth, extra care is needed; but when a living thing has time to mature, there is strength and security. Maturity moves us beyond selfish to selfless.

When the prodigal son decides to admit his sin and return home, he humbles himself. Humility is the opposite of pride. It is noble—putting your rights aside for the greater good of others. Humility will lead you to say powerful things: "I am sorry. I was wrong. Please forgive me. How can I make things better?"

As we take responsibility for our sins, we are forgiven and empowered to move forward in life. The first step is to come to our senses and acknowledge our mistakes. The second is to take responsibility for them by seeking forgiveness from our heavenly Father and those we've hurt.

Read Colossians 3:12-13 and Matthew 16:14-15 in the margin and answer the questions below.

According to these verses, why is it important to humble ourselves and seek forgiveness?

To whom do you need to say "I'm sorry"?

With whom do you need to seek forgiveness?

 12Therefore, as God's chosen people, holy and dearly loved, clothe yourselves with compassion, kindness, humility, gentleness and patience. 13Bear with each other and forgive one another if any of you has a grievance against someone. Forgive as the Lord forgave you.
(Colossians 3:12-13 NIV)

14"For if you forgive other people when they sin against you, your heavenly Father will also forgive you. 15But if you do not forgive others their sins, your Father will not forgive your sins."
(Matthew 6:14-15 NIV)

The deep and rich things of our faith are when we forgive those who hurt us, own and repent of our sins, run to restore broken relationships, and serve others in love.

How can you make things better with someone this week?

I often have people tell me they want to learn the deep stuff of the faith. They may say, "I just want to go deeper! Help me to move into the rich things of the faith." Friend, the deep stuff of the Christian faith is not learning Greek and Hebrew or knowing all the ancient traditions. The deep and rich things of our faith are when we forgive those who hurt us, own and repent of our sins, run to restore broken relationships, and serve others in love. This is the deep, hard, and meaningful work of the Christian life. May we together seek these deeper things!

Pray

- Spend a few minutes in silence simply focusing on God.
- Consider how Christ has modeled the fruit of the Spirit for you. Thank Him for His example.
- Ask God to help you cooperate with the Holy Spirit in order to strengthen the aspects of the fruit of the Spirit that you selected on page 46.

DAY 3: RUN TO RECONCILE

Settle

If the weather is nice, head outside today. Find a quiet spot and just be still for a few moments, enjoying God's presence in solitude. Or if that's not an option today, find a quiet space inside. Wherever you are, what sounds do you notice?

Focus

God shows his love for us in that while we were still sinners, Christ died for us.
(Romans 5:8 ESV)

"So he returned home to his father. And while he was still a long way off, his father saw him coming. Filled with love and compassion, he ran to his son, embraced him, and kissed him."

(Luke 15:20)

Review Luke 15:1-10.

Reflect

Recently, Jim and I had the opportunity to arrive a day early for a conference we were attending across the country. We had met one of the key speakers a few years ago and struck up a friendship. So in hopes of reconnecting, we sent a message that we were in town and hoped to see him before leaving town. Honestly, we figured he was really busy and might not even respond until after the event. To our surprise, he texted right back saying, "I'm at the venue. Come on over." We did.

As we approached the building, he saw us through a window and waved. That was nice, but what happened next was shocking.

He began to run. This well-known Christian leader stopped what he was doing and ran with his arms open to greet us about one hundred feet away. We were actually a little stunned at first, but three or four seconds into his run we thought, *Who cares who's watching; let's run too!*

In those few seconds, I had a flood of thoughts and emotions: *Is he running to us? There must be someone important behind us. Isn't he embarrassed? People are staring. I feel so special. This guy loves us. You know what, we love him too. Let's run!*

A few weeks later as Jim and I were standing in the lobby of our own home church, we saw a friend from another state approaching. We had not seen him in months. In a split second, Jim and I looked at each other, grinned, and broke into a run. He wrapped us up in a bear hug, and as we walked back to the lobby together I saw that a crowd had gathered, wondering what in the world would make us take off like that. In fact, one church member actually said, "I hope someone runs to me like that one day."

My takeaway? Run to people. Love them with abandon. It doesn't matter who is watching. Run, because love matters. We see this truth in the parable of the prodigal son.

Reread Luke 15:20 on page 49. What did the father do when he saw his son? How far away was the son?

In the Middle East at this time, men wore long garments that would have to be lifted in order to run, and it was unheard of for a man to do this. Running was for children. Showing your legs was disgraceful. So why run? Why not wait until his son has made it home and has given his speech? The son has practiced what he will say: "Father, I have sinned . . ." (Luke 15:18). Why not wait and have the prodigal show repentance and humility? After all, he has embarrassed his family. And having a son who has wasted wealth was actually punishable.

By Jewish custom, a young man who lost his family's inheritance in a foreign land and had the nerve to return to the village would be brought to justice through a custom called the *kezazah*, which means to be cut off.[1] When the community discovered the money was lost and the family had been disgraced, they would surround him and break a pot at his feet. This would indicate that he was cut off from the community—as if never having been born. The *kezazah* was a harsh tradition and one that a loving parent would not want to see their child forced to endure.

This father knows the tradition, and he isn't going to allow it. Even though his son has broken his heart, he has been watching and hoping for his son's return. He knows what will happen when the villagers see his boy. His son will be humiliated. The pot will be crushed, and his son will be lost to him forever. So before that can happen, the father does what no Middle

Eastern man in Jesus' day would do: he hikes up his robe and runs. Imagine the scene as you read the words again:

> And while he was still a long way off, his father saw him coming. Filled with love and compassion, he ran to his son, embraced him, and kissed him.
>
> (Luke 15:20)

Both father and son know the custom. The son has recognized his mistakes and is prepared to return in shame as a hired hand. But the wise father does not wait because he knows that unless he intervenes—unless he shows mercy; unless he disgraces himself by running in front of his servants, family, and village—the punishment will get to his son before his grace does. So he runs. And when he gets to his son, he embraces him, showering him with kisses. This display of love signals to everyone, especially his boy, that no pots will be broken here today!

Imagine you're one of the villagers. What do you feel as you see the father run?

Imagine you're the father. What do you feel as you run?

Imagine you're the son. What do you feel as you see your father running to you?

As we saw in Day 1, Jesus tells three stories of lost things in Luke 15. First there is the sheep that has gone astray, which the shepherd leaves his flock to go and find. Then there is the coin, which the woman diligently searches for until finding it. Finally there is the lost son, whom the father watches for, runs to, and redeems.

In my home I have a picture of a Middle Eastern shepherd with a large flock in his care. At one time I pictured myself as sheep number 702,983—just a random number in the flock. But through some healings in my heart, I came to realize I am not just one in the crowd but the one on the hillside.

I am the sheep that was a little lost but worth the shepherd's love and effort to find and restore. I was worth the search-and-rescue mission. My friend, you are too!

These parables, especially the one involving the running father, must have been shocking to the first-century audience. But Jesus' message was as clear to them as it should be to us today. Our heavenly Father has run to us through the humiliation of Jesus on the cross. He did not wait on us to come to Him but chose to run to us on a rescue mission by sending His Son, Jesus.

Read John 3:16-17 and Romans 5:8 in the margin.

What do these verses have to teach us about God's passionate pursuit of prodigal people?

Look again at Matthew 6:14-15, which we read yesterday (page 47). What do these verses teach us about our attitude toward others?

Through the cross and Jesus' resurrection, God ran to you.

When you are wronged, how quick are you to offer forgiveness and reconciliation? Do you tend to be a grudge holder? Explain your response.

Just as the father in our parable does not wait for his son to apologize, your heavenly Father has not waited for you to apologize. He acted first by sending Jesus. Through the cross and Jesus' resurrection, God ran to you. All you have to do is come home to Him to receive His embrace.

No matter what you've done or who you've hurt, God loves you. He loves you enough to send His Son so that He can have a relationship with you. He is not angry with you. He watches from a long way off, hoping to see you coming toward Him. And when He does, He runs to meet you!

Pray

- Song suggestion: "Mercy Came Running," recorded by Phillips, Craig and Dean.
- Perhaps you have been following Christ for decades. If so, thank God for His faithfulness in being a watchful Father. He has waited on you when you've been distant. He has searched for you when you've been lost. And He has run to you when you have called on Him. Thank Him for who He has been and continues to be in your life: a running Father!
- If you are not yet a Christ-follower, I hope you'll begin a journey with Him today. He knows you best and loves you most. You can pray the following prayer as printed or put it into your own words. God knows a sincere heart. Your words don't have to be perfect; just seek Him and ask Him to be in charge of your life:

God, I need You in my life. I accept Your Son, Jesus, as my Savior and want to allow Him to be Lord of my life. Please forgive me, cleanse me, and help me to follow You. Amen.

DAY 4: ALLOW FOR MISTAKES

Settle

Stand up and stretch for a minute or two. Take a few deep breaths and let your body relax. Now sit, settle in, and pause for a moment in silence before beginning your time with God today.

Focus

Make allowance for each other's faults, and forgive anyone who offends you. Remember, the Lord forgave you, so you must forgive others.

(Colossians 3:13)

[21]*"His son said to him, 'Father, I have sinned against both heaven and you, and I am no longer worthy of being called your son.'*

[22]*"But his father said to the servants, 'Quick! Bring the finest robe in the house and put it on him. Get a ring for his finger and sandals for his feet.* [23]*And kill the calf we have been fattening. We must celebrate with a feast,* [24]*for this son of mine was dead and has now returned to life. He was lost, but now he is found.' So the party began.*

[25]*"Meanwhile, the older son was in the fields working. When he returned home, he heard music and dancing in the house,* [26]*and he asked one of the servants what was going on.* [27]*'Your brother is back,' he was told, 'and your father has killed the fattened calf. We are celebrating because of his safe return.'*

[28]*"The older brother was angry and wouldn't go in. His father came out and begged him,* [29]*but he replied, 'All these years I've slaved for you and never once refused to do a single thing you told me to. And in all that time you never gave me even one young goat for a feast with my friends.* [30]*Yet when this son of yours comes back after squandering your money on prostitutes, you celebrate by killing the fattened calf!'"*

(Luke 15:21-30)

Reflect

When my daughter, Alyssa, was three, I went into my room to put on some lace-up boots only to find that the laces had been cut. I showed them to Alyssa and asked, "Do you know what happened to my boots?" She became very animated and said, "Oh, yes, it was a mouse." What? I stayed calm and said, "Well, tell me about that."

She said, "There was a mouse, and he did it; but it won't happen again, cuz I squished him." So I began to inquire where this squished mouse was. The trash? "Oh, no," she said, "because the mommy mouse came and dragged the baby mouse away." Okay, I thought, that was creative. "How did the mouse cut my laces?" I asked. "With his baby mouse scissors," was her reply. Now I'm thinking, Are you kidding me, kid?

At this point I'm getting ticked. It was the first time, to my knowledge, that my precious baby girl had ever lied. In fact, for a brief moment, I hoped that a mouse had done it—but the baby mouse scissors sealed the deal. My sweet girl had lied. She was a messy little person.

I sat Alyssa down on my lap and gently told her that she needed to tell me the truth, that making up stories was not okay. She stuck to her story without batting one of those beautiful long eyelashes. I did not know what to do. This was new, and I was mad.

I left the room, called Jim, and began to get hysterical. I believe my words to him when he said hello were, "She's a little liar. There was a mouse, and scissors, and the boots...sob, sob....What are we going to do? Why is she doing this? Where did this come from?" Once he could comprehend my emotional outburst, he said, "Well, she gets it from us, honey. We're sinners."

What would we do? She had lied. We would discipline her (no scissors for a month, and no play date for a week), and we would keep on loving her. We would forgive her. We would allow her to be human and make mistakes.

Reread Colossians 3:13 (page 54). What are we to do when others offend us, and why?

Have you ever been hurt by someone? I mean really wronged, hurt to the core? I have. And I'm guessing you have too. It's painful no matter where it comes from; but if it is someone close to us, the pain is even greater.

When someone hurts you, intentionally or not, how do you usually respond? What's your go-to emotion?

Perhaps you get ticked, as I did about Alyssa's mouse scissors. Or you might feel bitterness, discouragement, or even depression. Maybe you look for an opportunity to hurt them in return or take some sort of revenge. Or maybe you wait for them to come to you and make things right.

I've found all of these ways of responding useless! Bitterness and anger will eat you up. Discouragement and depression will leave you sad. Waiting for someone else to make things right is a waste of energy. The only person you really have control over is yourself. So determine in advance how you will respond when relationships get messy.

Read Ephesians 4:31-32 in the margin. What are we to avoid?

31Get rid of all bitterness, rage, anger, harsh words, and slander, as well as all types of evil behavior. 32Instead, be kind to each other, tenderhearted, forgiving one another, just as God through Christ has forgiven you.
(Ephesians 4:31-32)

What are some attitudes and actions we are to have toward others?

When we have been hurt, it is good to recall these verses on how to interact with others. A friend recently shared with me that when interacting with others, she strives to be direct, honest, and kind. She shared that we who follow Christ often start out kind; but when we become hurt or frustrated, we often go straight into "direct and honest" mode, which can become harsh and hurtful. Her life advice was to strive to live with all three: direct—going straight to the person we have an issue with; honest—dealing with the truth, no exaggeration; and kind—covering everything in love.

We simply do not have control over how others behave, but we do get to choose how we respond. Ephesians 4 gives us practical instructions: don't lose your cool, don't fly into a rage, no bad words or gossip. Instead, we are to do what simply does not come naturally at first: stay cool. We are to be compassionate and loving, offering forgiveness. This is what I call an

advanced maneuver. It takes practice and requires that we surrender our will to God. But the payoff is righteousness—the same kind of righteousness we see modeled in the father in the parable of the prodigal son.

As we have studied the parable this week, we have seen the younger son insult his father by taking an early inheritance and disgrace his family with wild living. But we also have seen him come to his senses, take responsibility for his actions, and ask for forgiveness. In response, his father not only runs to greet him and embrace him, forgiving him, but he also goes to great lengths to welcome his son home.

Reread Luke 15:22-24 (page 54). What does the father do to welcome his son?

What reason does he give in verse 24?

But while all of this is going on, there is another key character behind the scenes: the older son.

According to Luke 15:25 (page 54), what was the older son doing when his brother returned home?

What was his response to the news of the celebration?

What is this guy's deal? Why is he so angry? Perhaps he is embarrassed; surely the village has heard of his brother's wasteful spending and wild living. Perhaps he feels slighted and jealous when he learns of the party his dad is throwing. We don't know exactly what prompts his intense response, but Jesus makes it clear that the older brother was angry and resentful.

His little brother has acted terribly. He, on the other hand, has been faithful. Where is the justice? Instead of justice, there has been grace. Instead of a lecture there is love.

The secret for long-term healthy relationships: love each other deeply.

Try to put yourself in the older brother's shoes and be honest: how do you think you would have reacted?

When you feel hurt, do you long more for justice or grace?

Above all, love each other deeply, because love covers over a multitude of sins.

(1 Peter 4:8 NIV)

Read 1 Peter 4:8 in the margin. What does this verse instruct us to do, and why?

This beautiful verse contains the secret for long-term healthy relationships: love each other deeply. Sounds simple, right? As we know, simple is not always easy. But when we love deeply, we find strength to forgive. We find a way to get over our offense. We live into Colossians 3:13 and make allowance for the fact that those around us are not perfect. In fact, they, like us, are sinners—and sinners need forgiveness. Those who have hurt you need it, and you will need it again in the future too.

How have you experienced the truth of Colossians 3:13 and 1 Peter 4:8—on both the giving and the receiving ends? How have forgiveness and deep love affected your own life?

Let me say a word about what forgiveness is and what it is not. Too often we get this wrong. Forgiveness is not overlooking or condoning sin. It is not pretending that the hurt isn't real. That would be wrong. It is simply saying, "What happened is wrong, but I choose not to be angry and bitter about it. I choose to love you while still holding you accountable for your behavior."

We are held accountable for our sins, yet God offers us forgiveness through Christ. A clean slate that we have not earned and do not deserve. This is mercy. It is this mercy that the older brother does not show upon his sibling's return home.

Among the last words of Jesus spoken as he hung on the cross were, "Father, forgive them, for they don't know what they are doing" (Luke 23:34). Jesus came for messy people. He died for messy people. God loves really messy people.

When your relationships get messy, when you are hurt, be like the father in this story rather than the older brother. Run to those in need of forgiveness. Love deeply and make allowance for the faults of others. Forgive quickly and enjoy life. Go to the party!

Pray

- Song suggestion: "Forgiveness," recorded by Matthew West.
- Meditate on Ephesians 4:31-32 (NIV): "Get rid of all bitterness, rage and anger, brawling and slander, along with every form of malice. Be kind and compassionate to one another, forgiving each other, just as in Christ God forgave you."
- As you pray, express to God the freedom that you have felt through God's forgiveness of your sins.

DAY 5: SEEK PEACE

Settle

Sing or hum the familiar hymn "Amazing Grace." Let the lyrics "I once was lost, but now am found" seep into your soul and quiet the noises in your life for a few moments.

Focus

[31]"His father said to him, 'Look, dear son, you have always stayed by me, and everything I have is yours. [32]We had to celebrate this happy day. For your brother was dead and has come back to life! He was lost, but now he is found!' "

(Luke 15:31-32)

If it is possible, as far as it depends on you, live at peace with everyone.

(Romans 12:18 NIV)

Reflect

Early in my marriage, Jim and I had to learn to argue. I had never seen my parents fuss, so I just figured good marriages have no disagreements. (Turns out they were just private about their conflicts.) So as a new bride, the first time Jim got aggravated with me I thought, *Well, it's over.* We had a fight. He got loud, and I got historical. No, not hysterical. Historical. I began to lay out for him everything he had ever done that I didn't like. It was ridiculous. But if we were going to fight, then I wanted to win.

Then a wise friend gave me some valuable advice. She said, "Never aim to win an argument. If you win, then it means you made someone else a loser. And you don't want to make others losers. Always aim for the mutual win." I loved that. I really didn't want to make anyone a loser—especially not my sweet husband. I just had not learned how to handle conflict.

Over the years I have tried to apply that advice to all of my relationships. I don't want to win, even when I'm right, if it means that others become losers. That's just mean. Can you be right and mean? Absolutely. Can you tell the truth and be a jerk? Definitely. But don't do it. Instead, aim for a mutual win.

Reread Romans 12:18 on page 60, and rewrite the verse in your own words below:

Does this mean that you cave in on every disagreement? No. It means you change how you approach things. You seek to understand and then be understood. You learn to control your attitude, tone, timing, and temper. You learn to express yourself in ways that speak truth without putting anyone down. Above all, it requires humility to seek the mutual win instead of the personal one.

Consider what those around you would say about how well you control each of these four elements of disagreement, putting a check mark in the appropriate column:

	Great	Good	Meh	Terrible
1. Attitude				
2. Tone				
3. Timing				
4. Temper				

> It requires humility to seek the mutual win instead of the personal one.

Over the years I have learned to control my tone and temper pretty well, but timing and attitude tend to be a moving target for me. I like quick resolution. Having to wait for the right moment and setting sometimes can feel like an eternity to me. But I am learning that there is great wisdom in choosing timing well. And as for attitude, my face betrays me no matter my tone. Knowing that, I have to be intentional to get right with God and have good motives before speaking.

What about you? Which of these do you struggle with? Once you identify your weak areas, you can become intentional in how you approach others.

Romans 14:19 in *The Message* reads, "Let's agree to use all our energy in getting along with each other. Help others with encouraging words; don't drag them down by finding fault." Part of being human is dealing with relationships when they get messy. When there is hurt, betrayal, and disappointment, we get to choose how we will respond. Learning good communication skills and going out of our way to develop healthy patterns in dealing with others is a burden that the Christ-follower must bear in order to serve Jesus well.

[34]"So now I am giving you a new commandment: Love each other. Just as I have loved you, you should love each other. [35]Your love for one another will prove to the world that you are my disciples."

(John 13:34-35)

Read John 13:34-35 in the margin. What are Jesus' instructions to those who follow Him?

How would you describe what it means to love as Jesus loved? Practically speaking, what does this look like?

Love builds bridges. I recently read that it is estimated that nearly 56,000 bridges in the United States are structurally deficient.[2] Although still in operation, they simply are not safe. As I read that statistic, I thought about how we need bridges of trust and forgiveness to get past deficiencies in relationships. In other words, without trust and forgiveness as part of its foundation, a relationship is simply not strong enough to endure the heavy loads that life sometimes brings.

We need bridges of trust and forgiveness to get past deficiencies in relationships.

Which relationships in your life are structurally deficient right now?

How can you begin to repair and reinforce those bridges of relationships?

Through our study this week we have taken a look at five key steps in restoring messy relationships, which are listed on the following page. Notice that each one begins with a verb. The verbs emphasize the fact that you can take action steps in the healing process.

1. **Come** to your senses—by seeking God's will and acknowledging your part in broken relationships.
2. **Take** responsibility—by repenting of your sins and commiting to make things right.
3. **Run** to reconcile—taking the first step toward forgiveness.
4. **Allow** for mistakes—by loving others deeply.
5. **Seek** peace—by using your energy to build others up and strengthen relationships.

Which of these five action steps do you most need to activate today? Circle it above. Then write below how you can begin to implement this action step in your life:

The parable of the prodigal son is actually a story of two lost boys. First there is the prodigal, the younger son who wastes his inheritance on living a wild life. And then there is the older brother, who is angry that there is celebration for his sinful sibling. In both situations we see a father who seeks what is lost. Just as the shepherd who searches for his lost sheep and the woman who cleans until she finds her valuable coin (Luke 15:4-10), this loving father is proactive in reaching out to his lost sons. We don't see him hesitate to love both of his boys deeply.

Consider once again the father's attitude in these verses, and describe in your own words how his actions reveal his deep love for each son:

"And while he was still a long way off, his father saw him coming. Filled with love and compassion, he ran to his son, embraced him, and kissed him."

(Luke 15:20)

How his actions reveal his deep love for the younger son:

28"The older brother was angry and wouldn't go in. His father came out and begged him, . . . 31"Look, dear son, you have always stayed by me, and everything I have is yours. 32We had to celebrate this happy day. For your brother was dead and has come back to life! He was lost, but now he is found!' "

(Luke 15:28, 31-32)

How his actions reveal his deep love for the older son:

A loving father, a prodigal son, and a resentful brother: which do you most relate to today? Why?

Hebrews 12:14 tells us, "Work at living in peace with everyone, and work at living a holy life, for those who are not holy will not see the Lord."

There are several characters in this parable, but by far the noble one is the father who runs to reconcile the relationship—a parent who had been disappointed, hurt, humiliated, scared, and surely at times angry. But he ran! Friend, let's resolve not to be the prodigal, who was caught up in wild living, or the older brother, who was judgmental and cold. Let us be the ones who run to restore what was broken. And as we do, may it bring a smile to God's face!

Pray

- As you consider those with whom you need to seek peace, imagine that you're sitting with Jesus discussing the situation. Invite Him to speak to you in prayer. What does He suggest you do?
- What is keeping you from taking those steps? Pray through those obstacles.
- Thank God for His goodness in your life today and every day.

VIDEO VIEWER GUIDE: WEEK 2

"For the Son of Man came to seek and to save the lost."

(Luke 19:10 NIV)

"When he finally came to his senses, he said to himself, 'At home even the hired servants have food enough to spare, and here I am dying of hunger!' "

(Luke 15:17)

1. Make the _____ _____.

Do all that you can to live in peace with everyone.

(Romans 12:18)

"So if you are presenting a sacrifice at the altar in the Temple and you suddenly remember that someone has something against you, leave your sacrifice there at the altar. Go and be reconciled to that person. Then come and offer your sacrifice to God."

(Matthew 5:23-24)

2. Own our _____.

"Why do you notice the little piece of dust in your friend's eye, but you don't notice the big piece of wood in your own eye? . . . First, take the wood out of your own eye. Then you will see clearly to take the dust out of your friend's eye."

(Matthew 7:3-5 NCV)

3. Listen _____.

Everyone should be quick to listen, slow to speak and slow to become angry.

(James 1:19 NIV)

4. Speak _____.

The words of the reckless pierce like swords,
    but the tongue of the wise brings healing.
        (Proverbs 12:18 NIV)

Do not use harmful words, but only helpful words, the kind that build up.
        (Ephesians 4:29 GNT)

5. Focus on _____ and not just _____.

Week 3

Josiah

Breaking Messy Family Cycles

2 Kings 22–23;
2 Chronicles 34–35

DAY 1: EXAMINING YOUR LIFE

Settle

Find a quiet spot, be still for a moment, and then pray, offering this Scripture to God as a means of settling your Spirit:

²³*Search me, O God, and know my heart;*
   test me and know my anxious thoughts.
²⁴*Point out anything in me that offends you,*
   and lead me along the path of everlasting life.
                          (Psalm 139:23-24)

Focus

Instead, let us test and examine our ways.
   Let us turn back to the LORD.
            (Lamentations 3:40)

¹*Josiah was eight years old when he became king, and he reigned in Jerusalem thirty-one years.* ²*He did what was right in the eyes of the LORD and followed the ways of his father David, not turning aside to the right or to the left.*

³*In the eighth year of his reign, while he was still young, he began to seek the God of his father David. In his twelfth year he began to purge Judah and Jerusalem of high places, Asherah poles and idols....*

⁸*In the eighteenth year of Josiah's reign, to purify the land and the temple, he sent Shaphan son of Azaliah and Maaseiah the ruler of the city, with Joah son of Joahaz, the recorder, to repair the temple of the LORD his God.*
                          (2 Chronicles 34:1-3, 8 NIV)

Read more of Josiah's story in 2 Chronicles 34 and 35.

Reflect

The door to my son's room is usually closed. And that's fine with me because I know that behind that door, most of the time, are dirty clothes, an unmade bed, abandoned late-night snacks, and, honestly, who knows what else. But what I didn't realize until recently is what was deeper within the

When we take time to sort through life's messes and put things in order, the future holds the promise of new blessings.

room, waiting inside his walk-in closet. One day as I opened Josh's closet door, I saw piles of clothes, spilled airsoft BBs from his middle school days, notebooks from three years ago, and a suitcase still packed with clothes from a previous football camp. So I did what came easiest; I just closed the door. And then I waited, hoping that he would take the initiative and clean up that mess! He didn't. So I helped that process along.

I'm not that mom who gets really mad about stuff like that, but I did tell him very clearly to clean up that mess. And he did, sort of. It was better, but it was still a mess. Honestly, for that closet to be really clean, it was going to take a major effort. It was not going to be fun or pleasant. So we made it a team project and worked on it together. We had to get in there and pick through every pile, examine every box, and go through each bag. It took time, and it was a bit yucky.

No discipline seems pleasant at the time, but painful. Later on, however, it produces a harvest of righteousness and peace for those who have been trained by it. (Hebrews 12:11 NIV)

Read Hebrews 12:11 in the margin. How does this verse describe discipline and its results?

Not long after cleaning out and organizing that closet, Josh remarked that life sure was easier with things in their right order. That struck me as a profound thought. Life really is much easier when we take time to examine the state of things and then put them in the right order. But it's easy to get off track and end up with a mess. If we just "close the door" and ignore the mess, it won't go away—and might even become worse with time.

Life is full of messes. But when we take time to sort through life's messes and put things in order, the future holds the promise of new blessings.

Reread Lamentations 3:40 (page 69). What do you think it means to "test and examine our ways"?

How might this help us to turn back to the Lord?

This week we are going to consider the process of examining our lives, including messy family cycles, as we dig into the life of one of the youngest and best kings of the Old Testament, Josiah. Interestingly, he was the son and grandson of two of the worst kings in Judah's history, Amon and Manasseh, who brought idolatry, pagan sacrifice, and witchcraft to God's people. After the assassination of his father when Josiah was only eight years old, he inherited the throne and found himself the king of a nation in serious trouble.

Josiah could have repeated the destructive patterns handed down to him, but he chose to change the direction of his life and his country. Josiah's legacy includes cleansing the country of pagan practices and renewing the people's covenant with God. With the help of godly advisors, Josiah led his nation back to God through repentance. He truly is counted a hero of the Israelites.

But before any of that happened, Josiah was born into a mess. It was only through obedience and dedication that he was able to lead an entire nation back into favor with God. As we study his life this week, we will see that he had to make intentional decisions in order to live in new ways pleasing to the Lord.

What messes have been passed on to you?

How have they impacted your life to this point?

We read in 2 Chronicles 34 that after Josiah had reigned for eight years, when he was sixteen years old, he began to seek the God of his father David (which means forefather or ancestor); and within just a few years his devotion was evident to all.

Look again at 2 Chronicles 34:3 (page 69). What did Josiah begin to do in the twelfth year of his reign?

Just for fun, do the math. How old would he have been then?

As a teenager Josiah began to seek God in earnest. He examined the situation that Judah now faced. The country was entrenched in idolatry and pagan worship. Josiah realized that he must lead his country back to the God of the great King David—back to holiness. In 2 Chronicles 34:4-7, we read that Josiah tore down the altars to Baal, smashed the Asherah poles, and broke all the idols that the people were worshiping. He took action to end the false worship and began to lead his people back toward God.

According to 2 Chronicles 34:8 (page 69), what did Josiah do in the eighteenth year of his reign?

Do the math one more time. How old was he then?

After cleansing the land of its idols, Josiah began the process of rebuilding the temple of the one true God. During the building, a great discovery was made. The Book of the Law, God's Word, was found. Imagine that: the people of God had abandoned and lost God's Word! Upon hearing God's commands read aloud, Josiah was deeply moved.

When the king heard the words of the Law, he tore his robes.

(2 Chronicles 34:19 NIV)

Read 2 Chronicles 34:19 in the margin. What did Josiah do when he heard the words of the Law?

Josiah "tore his robes" as a sign of his grief over how far from God's will Judah had strayed. And as we read in 2 Kings 23, he gathered all of his people "from the least to the greatest" and read to them what was contained in the Book of the Covenant, leading the people in national repentance and into a right relationship with God (vv. 1-3). Scripture tells us, "As long as he lived, they did not fail to follow the LORD, the God of their ancestors" (2 Chronicles 34:33).

God's people had abandoned Him. They literally had lost God's Word and had fallen into all types of depravity. But with the help of God's Spirit and good counsel, Josiah examined the state of his country and determined to return things to their right order.

The examples that had been set for Josiah were poor ones. His father and grandfather had not honored the Lord. But Josiah looked beyond what he knew as normal to examine the values and practices within his culture. Then as God's Word was revealed to him, he made the decisions necessary to put things back into right order. Josiah led his people through a process of national repentance in which they renewed their covenant to the Lord. As a result, throughout Josiah's lifetime the people of Judah honored God and served Him only.

Now, let's bring this home into our lives.

Socrates, the great philosopher, is credited with saying, "An unexamined life is not worth living." Though every life has value, the idea here is that a fulfilling life is an examined life. There are many Scriptures that affirm this idea.

Read the following Scriptures, and note what insight each gives related to the practice of personal examination:

²³Search me, O God, and know my heart;
test me and know my anxious thoughts.
²⁴Point out anything in me that offends you,
and lead me along the path of everlasting life.
(Psalm 139:23-24)

How many wrongs and sins have I committed?
Show me my offense and my sin.
(Job 13:23 NIV)

I considered my ways
And turned my feet to Your testimonies.
(Psalm 119:59 NASB)

Do you not realize that Christ Jesus is in you—unless, of course, you fail the test?

(2 Corinthians 13:5 NIV)

As Christ-followers, those of us who do not discipline ourselves by routinely evaluating our life choices are like the unattended garden where weeds gather and choke out the blooms, or the closet where clutter gathers and leaves the space unusable. Life is messy, but by honestly and routinely examining every nook and cranny of our attitudes and behaviors, we can build lives of beauty and purpose.

Examine your life in the following areas. Circle those where you are doing well. Underline those that need attention.

Habits	**Prayer Life**	**Attitude**
Language	**Work Ethic**	**Honesty**
Patience	**Mood Swings**	**Kindness**
Bible Study	**Serving Others**	**Career**
Relationships	**Physical Fitness**	**Sharing Your Faith**

Financial Responsibility

Now take a look at what you've just underlined. Pick one or two areas to concentrate on, and begin today to be proactive in moving forward in these areas. If you have no idea where to start, then seek help. But most likely, you already know a first step. If you underlined financial responsibility, for example, you might make a budget and start keeping all receipts. If your goal is kindness, you might choose today to do three intentional acts to express kindness. If it's physical fitness, you might take a walk and cut out the cookies. But whatever you do, do it today.

As you begin to work on areas needing your attention, allow this to motivate you to have a plan and set new goals. Like Josiah, examine your situation and resolve to make a difference. If you start today and are faithful, by the end of this study you may find you have developed some new healthy habits in which you can be proud.

Today our focus has been on learning from Josiah the importance of examining our lives and repenting of areas that are not pleasing to God. The rest of this week we will continue learning from his example about overcoming excuses that hold us back, taking first steps and surrendering control to God, defeating destructive patterns that would lead us back into temptation, and building a team to support us as we move closer to Christ.

Like Josiah, you may have things that have been passed on to you that make holy living a challenge. But also like Josiah, you can move beyond these challenges with God's help. My prayer is that this week we all will honestly examine our own situations and move past anything holding us back from God's very best!

Pray

- Song suggestion: "The Comeback," recorded by Danny Gokey. (As you listen, prayerfully consider what it will take for you to overcome obstacles in your path.)
- Examine your life and repent of any areas of unfaithfulness to God.
- Praise God for how He is there for you when you seek Him.

DAY 2: OVERCOMING EXCUSES

Settle

Take just five minutes to express your love for God through music, art, writing, or some other creative outlet. As you create, allow God's presence to penetrate your current situation.

Focus

Let us strip off every weight that slows us down, especially the sin that so easily trips us up.

(Hebrews 12:1b)

[21] Amon [Josiah's father] was twenty-two years old when he became king, and he reigned in Jerusalem two years. [22] He did what was evil in the LORD's sight, just as his father, Manasseh, had done. He worshiped and sacrificed to all the idols his father had made. [23] But unlike his father, he did not humble himself before the LORD. Instead, Amon sinned even more.

(2 Chronicles 33:21-23)

[1] Josiah was eight years old when he became king, and he reigned in Jerusalem thirty-one years. [2] He did what was right in the eyes of the LORD and followed the ways of his father David, not turning aside to the right or to the left.

[3] In the eighth year of his reign, while he was still young, he began to seek the God of his father David. In his twelfth year he began to purge Judah and Jerusalem of high places, Asherah poles and idols. . . .

[8] In the eighteenth year of Josiah's reign, to purify the land and the temple, he sent Shaphan son of Azaliah and Maaseiah the ruler of the city, with Joah son of Joahaz, the recorder, to repair the temple of the LORD his God.

(2 Chronicles 34:1-3, 8 NIV)

Reflect

So let's get personal. Do you have a bad habit? I do. Sometimes it really doesn't even seem that bad to me. I justify it by telling myself that at least it's not porn or lust; it's not greed, infidelity, or theft. But I know it's hurting my quality of life and affecting my family too. And that means it is a problem in my life. So here it is. One of my worst habits is also one of my favorite things: ice cream! Well, if I'm being honest, it's food in general and sweets in particular. They're awesome!

I know it's not the best thing for me. Yes, losing weight would be great, planning meals in advance would be beneficial, and avoiding sugary foods would help. But . . . my life is very busy. The schedule is usually hectic, and the to-do list is lengthy. So when it comes to meal planning and cooking, I'm not very diligent. Instead, we often eat on the run. This has become not only my bad habit but also one that I have passed on to my children.

Recently when I was explaining why it is so hard for me to plan healthy meals, I was struck with the realization that I was just making excuses. The things I mentioned were real obstacles, but they were my excuses for not taking the time and energy to do what I need to do for my family's health. For me to get this under control, I realized I needed to change the way I think about nutrition and time management. Instead of excuses, I needed a plan.

I'm not alone as an excuse maker. The Bible has many famous people who also made excuses for why they couldn't live into God's best for them. Adam and Eve were the first. In Genesis 3, after disobeying God by eating the fruit from the Tree of Life, Adam blamed Eve and Eve blamed the serpent. Then in Exodus 3, Moses famously had one excuse after another why God should not use him to lead the Hebrews out of slavery in Egypt. And in Judges 6, Gideon felt he was too young and poor to be used to lead Israel against the Midianites.

Oh, how tired God must get of listening to our excuses! It's so easy to be overwhelmed with our fears and inadequacies instead of being strengthened by our faith in God and the knowledge that His power is at work in our lives.

Read Ephesians 6:10 in the margin. What makes us strong? How does this verse apply to our messes and bad habits?

Instead of trying harder, making excuses, or buying a self-help book, we can turn to the Lord with our messes and rely on Him to help us.

Now it's your turn. What's your bad habit?

> **Instead of trying harder, making excuses, or buying a self-help book, we can turn to the Lord with our messes and rely on Him to help us.**

> *Be strong in the Lord and in his mighty power. (Ephesians 6:10 NIV)*

How does it affect your life and those around you?

How does it affect your testimony as a follower of Christ?

What's your excuse for why you don't break this habit?

Discipline yourself for the purpose of godliness.

(1 Timothy 4:7b NASB)

Take time and trouble to keep yourself spiritually fit.

(1 Timothy 4:7b JBP)

Read the two translations of 1 Timothy 4:7b in the margin, and consider how this verse might direct your daily life. Record any thoughts below:

God's Word tells us that we are to be disciplined and do what is necessary to live in ways that honor Him. We are to move past our excuses into obedience. We are to lean on God's strength in our weakness.

Yesterday we began the journey of a careful examination of our lives. That first step of examination helps us determine what we need to work on. Next, we have to overcome the temptation to make excuses for why we are stuck in these unhealthy patterns and ungodly habits. First Corinthians 10:13 tells us, "No temptation has overtaken you except what is common to mankind. And God is faithful; he will not let you be tempted beyond what you can bear. But when you are tempted, he will also provide a way out so that you can endure it" (NIV). In other words, no excuses accepted! "I will help you," God says.

As we read yesterday, young Josiah grew up in an ungodly household. According to Scripture, his granddad Manasseh was one of the most evil kings in the history of Judah. Josiah's father, Amon, followed that example. Then at eight years old, Josiah found himself in charge. He had had no godly role models in his family. Idol worship had overcome the nation, and his country was a big, unholy mess. The problems must have seemed overwhelming.

It would have been easy for him to come up with excuses for why he was not up to the job of kingdom reformation. He could have blamed his parents or the state of the nation as he found it. He could have said, "I'm just a boy." But he didn't. Instead, as we've seen, he sought the one true God, removed the pagan idols, and rebuilt the temple for worship. He personally recommitted himself to God and then led his entire nation to do the same. For Josiah, there were no excuses.

Sometimes our excuses become the tool that allows us to rationalize poor behavior and settle for less than God's best in our lives. These bad habits often fall into the category of sin.

Look back at Hebrews 12:1 (page 76). What word is used to describe what slows us down, including sin?

The word used here is *weight*. A weight is anything that slows us down. It could be a habit, a relationship, or our schedule. Sometimes the weights that slow us down aren't bad things but good things that have gotten out of balance and now, instead of helping us, are dragging us down.

Now consider the phrase "including sin." Obviously, sin in our lives is a weight or obstacle that prevents us from seeing God's best for us. Another way of thinking about sin is anything that contradicts or leads us away from God's will or desire for us. For example, Mr. Right won't come along while you're dating Mr. Wrong. The kids are likely not to pursue godly lives if that isn't what is modeled at home. And you won't lose weight eating on the run—or at least I haven't. God does not bless disobedience.

As you think about the bad habit you named earlier, answer these questions honestly:

How long has this been an issue in your life?

Are you ready to deal with it once and for all?

Ephesians 4:14-15 teaches us that we are not meant to remain as children but are to grow up in every way into Christ. Part of growing up is accepting responsibility for our lives and our own mistakes and shortcomings.

"Learn to be mature."
(Proverbs 8:5 GNT)

Read Proverbs 8:5 in the margin and circle the verb used in this verse.

When we learn a new skill or develop a new habit, there is a learning curve. It's during that time that we have to be the most disciplined and determined. As we examine our lives and seek the steps we need to take to move toward holiness, we must get rid of anything that would hold us back. No excuses.

Like Josiah, each of us must take an honest look at our situation and then move past whatever has held us back in the past in order to live our best and richest lives in God's grace and favor!

Pray

- Just as you identified your excuse for not breaking your bad habit, make a list of the excuses that have held you back from following God wholeheartedly.
- Now tear up that list! Ask God to help you overcome and move past excuses that are holding you back from pursuing His will in your life.
- If you're able, go into a kneeling position and seek God's power to move into a new level of fellowship with Him today.

DAY 3: TAKING FIRST STEPS

Settle

If possible, find a new spot today for your time with God. Mix it up a little so that you stay alert and fresh as you enter into God's presence.

Focus

Surrender yourself to the LORD, and wait patiently for him.

(Psalm 37:7 GW)

[4]He [Josiah] ordered that the altars of Baal be demolished and that the incense altars which stood above them be broken down. He also made sure that the Asherah poles, the carved idols, and the cast images were smashed and scattered over the graves of those who had sacrificed to them. [5]He burned the bones of the pagan priests on their own altars, and so he purified Judah and Jerusalem.

(2 Chronicles 34:4-5)

Reflect

After ten years in ministry, my husband, Jim, asked me to join him in quitting our jobs and moving to a new area to start a church. It didn't make sense to me. We had great jobs and successful ministries. Why move to an area where we knew no one? There was no church building, no land, no launch team, and no guarantee of success. We had a two-year-old and a baby on the way. Overall, this seemed like a terrible plan to me.

But Jim was convinced that God was leading him to do this. And then he made this statement: "Jen, I know God is leading me to start a church, but if you are not 100 percent on board, I'll walk away." I appreciated that, but what pressure!

During that time, God revealed Himself to me in several ways, but one was simply through these familiar verses from the story of Abram and Sarai:

[1]The LORD had said to Abram, "Go from your country, your people and your father's household to the land I will show you.

[2]"I will make you into a great nation,
   and I will bless you; . . ."

[4]So Abram went, as the LORD had told him; . . . [5]He took his wife Sarai.

(Genesis 12:1-2, 4-5 NIV)

As I reread these verses, what jumped out at me this time was that the Lord told Abraham what to do and he did it—and his wife went with him. Also, they went with the promise of blessing. It was simple availability, obedience, and trust. But simple is not always easy.

I felt God moving us to start this new church. If I'm honest, I still had two main fears: (1) What if we fail? (2) What if we run out of money? These were real possibilities. However, I knew that, like Abram and Sarai, I had to be obedient without knowing what the future held. I had to surrender everything—my career, my income, my stability, and my trust—into God's hands.

So while sitting with Jim on a beach, pondering God's vast greatness, I finally looked at him and said, "I'm in." We didn't know what the future held, but we wanted to be in on whatever God was going to do. It was one of the scariest, most rewarding decisions I have ever made.

How have you felt God calling you in the past?

Every day you decide who will be in control of your life. Will it be you or God?

On Day 1 we took the time to examine our lives and identify what messes are holding us back in life. Yesterday we confronted our excuses that perpetuate the cycle of being stuck in this mess. Today we are going to do something about it!

Let's consider a couple of first steps we must take in order to follow God's plan for our lives.

1. Give up control.

First, we must give up! That may sound like inaction, but actually it is the critical first step we must take. Psalm 37:7 tells us to surrender ourselves to the Lord and wait patiently for Him. Giving up control is hard. Most of us like things done our way and on our timetable. Surrendering our plans for God's plans can be scary. In fact, most of us work hard to stay in control and on top of things. Then we read a Scripture like Psalm 37:7 and think, "But God, if I give up control, everything will fall apart!" Have you ever felt that way?

Read Psalm 46:10 in the margin. What are we to let go of, and what will be the result when we do?

Every day you decide who will be in control of your life. Will it be you or God? God has the bigger picture of your life in mind. He sees things that you cannot see and wants to guide you in ways that you cannot yet understand. His plans are better than yours, just as they are better than mine. The question is, will you trust that He is looking out for you even when you can't understand all that is happening in your life?

Read Isaiah 55:8-9 in the margin. How does this verse give you wisdom or comfort for those times when you can't understand what is happening in your life?

The payoffs of surrender are many. First, you will find that you worry less and trust more. You can trust that God's plan is sufficient for all of your needs, that He will provide when you can't figure things out. You also will reap the benefits of life in obedience to God's will. Through that obedience you will feel much less stress once you are relieved from trying to control people and situations. That stress can take a toll on you physically, with tangible symptoms such as high blood pressure, obesity, diabetes, and heart disease. Through surrender, those issues or risks can be greatly reduced. And of course, there is the benefit of close fellowship with your heavenly Father.

John 14:21 encourages us to surrender and obey God by reminding us, "Those who accept my commandments and obey them are the ones who love me. And because they love me, my Father will love them. And I will love them and reveal myself to each of them." Notice in this verse there is a premise and a promise. The premise is to accept and obey God's commands. The promise is that God will reveal Himself.

Is there an area of your life that you have withheld from God's control? If so, what is it?

Let go of your concerns!
Then you will know that I am God.
I rule the nations.
I rule the earth.
(Psalm 46:10 GW)

8"For my thoughts are not your thoughts,
neither are your ways my ways,"
declares the LORD.
9"As the heavens are higher than the earth,
so are my ways higher than your ways
and my thoughts than your thoughts."
(Isaiah 55:8-9 NIV)

In the past when you have surrendered control to God, what have been the effects on you physically, emotionally, mentally, and spiritually?

As we surrender our will to God's, we take the necessary first step in taking part in His plan for our lives. This can be challenging, though, because surrender doesn't come naturally for most of us, does it? What comes naturally to me is wanting to control my situation. This is where we have to trust and obey. Like Abram and Sarai, we follow God's leading without knowing exactly where He is leading us. Scary, but worth it!

2. Get started!

Once we surrender control to God and say yes to His plan, we must simply take action! This may seem like a no-brainer, but so often we procrastinate because of fear. What fears keep you from God's plans? Perhaps it's a fear of failure, the unknown, a lifestyle change, or criticism. Move past those fears in faith. Trust God even when the way does not seem perfectly clear. As we read in Ecclesiastes, "If you wait for perfect conditions, you will never get anything done" (11:4 TLB).

If you look for a reason to delay following God's will, you will find it every time. As we learned yesterday, there will always be an excuse to continue in sin or delay obedience or put off following a dream. For instance:

When I have more money, then I'll tithe.
When work settles down, then I'll take better care of myself.
When the kids are older, then I'll have time for God/God's plan.

The best day to get started living into God's will for your life is today!

If Jim and I had waited for a launch team, enough money, the kids to be older, or all of our family to be supportive, we never would have started the church. We launched a church in a band room at a school. It was not ideal, but it was a start; and from there, God led us into bigger and better opportunities. The hard part was just getting started.

There is a time to plan—a time to strategize, pray, and learn. But there also is a time to move. As you pursue dreams, take the time to learn, gather wise counsel, develop a plan, and establish time lines; but don't be too afraid to get started. Far too many dreams die in the waiting stage. Don't allow the desire for perfection to become fuel for procrastination. We live in a less-than-perfect world, so we are forced to follow God in less-than-perfect circumstances. Do it anyway!

If you knew you wouldn't fail, what would you attempt for God's glory in your life?

The best day to get started living into God's will for your life is today!

We see the steps of surrender and action in Josiah's life. As we've learned in our study this week, Josiah was born into a difficult situation. His father and grandfather had led Judah into idolatry and witchcraft, but he sought a better path. Through Josiah's passionate leadership, the people of Judah left their pagan practices and renewed their covenant with God.

This could not have been wildly popular among all the people of Judah at first. For decades they had worshiped idols. There were pagan priests dedicated to that form of worship. But Josiah's surrender to God was unconditional. So, as a young man, he started ridding the country of idolatry and taking practical steps to lead his people to God.

I look back at the younger me sitting on that beach, and I feel for her. She was so scared. Sometimes I wish I could go back and reassure my younger self. I'd say something like, "Girl, listen, you are not going to believe what God is going to do when you step out in faith. Don't be afraid. Just do it! This will be one of the greatest journeys of your life!" But you know, on second thought, maybe I wouldn't tell her that at all. Because maybe she needed to face those fears, surrender everything to God, and step out in that fear not knowing what the future held.

God has a good and fruitful plan for your life, my friend. Give all of who you are to God, and start living into His best for you!

Pray

- There's an old hymn that says, "Count your many blessings, name them one by one." Take the time to list some of the blessings God has brought into your life. Thank God for these blessings and for caring about the details of your life.
- Ask God for clarity about next steps in following the dreams He has planted in your heart.
- Now pray in faith for the courage to take the first steps in pursuing God's best plan for you. Surrender control and get started!

DAY 4: DEFEATING DESTRUCTIVE PATTERNS

Settle

As you settle into your time with God, listen to some music that soothes your spirit. You might try "What a Beautiful Name," recorded by Hillsong Worship.

Focus

So I say, let the Holy Spirit guide your lives. Then you won't be doing what your sinful nature craves.

(Galatians 5:16)

[14]*Hilkiah the priest found the Book of the Law of the LORD that was written by Moses.* [15]*Hilkiah said to Shaphan the court secretary, "I have found the Book of the Law in the LORD's Temple!" Then Hilkiah gave the scroll to Shaphan....*

[18]*Shaphan also told the king, "Hilkiah the priest has given me a scroll." So Shaphan read it to the king.*

[19]*When the king heard what was written in the Law, he tore his clothes in despair.* [20]*Then he gave these orders to Hilkiah, Ahikam son of Shaphan, Acbor son of Micaiah, Shaphan the court secretary, and Asaiah the king's personal adviser:* [21]*"Go to the Temple and speak to the LORD for me and for all the remnant of Israel and Judah. Inquire about the words written in the scroll that has been found. For the LORD's great anger has been poured out on us because our ancestors have not obeyed the word of the LORD. We have not been doing everything this scroll says we must do."...*

[29]*Then the king summoned all the elders of Judah and Jerusalem....* [30]*all the people from the greatest to the least. There the king read to them the entire Book of the Covenant that had been found in the LORD's Temple.* [31]*...He pledged to obey the LORD by keeping all his commands, laws, and decrees with all his heart and soul....* [32]*And he required everyone in Jerusalem and the people of Benjamin to make a similar pledge.*

(2 Chronicles 34:14-15, 18-21, 29-32)

Reflect

My husband, Jim, has a dear friend whom we see only once every five years or so. When we were first married, he came to visit; and I made lasagna. We had a great visit until he began to break out into a hard sweat during dinner. I tried to ignore it at first and then realized he was really in distress. Wanting to be polite, he ate the meal set before him, although he was allergic to tomatoes. I felt terrible.

Fast forward a few years. He and his new wife came to see us, and I prepared dinner. Not lasagna, though. Instead, I made spaghetti! I forgot completely about the allergy, until the sweating started. Ugh!

I hate to make mistakes. I really hate to repeat the same mistakes. It seems so stupid and such a waste of time. But it happens.

The nation of Israel had a habit of making the same mistakes again and again. As we've seen, young King Josiah found himself the head of a nation that was entrenched in idolatry. This was not the first time the Israelites had faced the crisis of unfaithfulness. There were many other kings such as Jehoram and Ahaziah (2 Chronicles 21–22) who had led God's people in detestable ways away from the Lord and into idol worship and pagan practices. Why hadn't Manasseh and Amon, Josiah's grandfather and father, learned from the lessons of those who went before them? Instead of effecting positive change, they repeated the same mistakes that had cost Israel so dearly throughout the ages and then handed this sinful nation to Josiah to rule.

In fact, God's people had strayed so far from the Lord that they literally had misplaced God's Word! When Hilkiah, the priest, found the lost Scriptures in the temple, they were taken to King Josiah and read to him. As Josiah heard them read, he became brokenhearted that God's people had wandered so far away from God's plan for them. But Josiah didn't just stay brokenhearted. He took action and recommitted to the principles of God found in Scripture.

Josiah chose to break the pattern. He did not want to repeat the same sins of his ancestors. He not only had the courage to confront sin and break the patterns of sin in his family and country; he also encouraged them to return wholeheartedly to obeying God's instructions. What a great life lesson for us today. God's Word is meant to be a road map, a guide toward wisdom and living into God's favor. One of my favorite verses is Psalm 119:9 (GNT), which reads, "How can young people keep their lives pure? / By obeying your

> **God's Word is meant to be a road map, a guide toward wisdom and living into God's favor.**

15I don't really understand myself, for I want to do what is right, but I don't do it. Instead, I do what I hate....

17So I am not the one doing wrong; it is sin living in me that does it.

18And I know that nothing good lives in me, that is, in my sinful nature. I want to do what is right, but I can't....

(Romans 7:15, 17-18)

commands." How can we live in a way that pleases the Lord? By knowing and obeying the Bible.

In the Book of Job we read, "The longer you live, the wiser you become" (32:7 MSG). But this is not a promise; it is a possibility. Some people live longer and just become older, not wiser. Wisdom comes from God. It's possible to repeat the same mistakes, stay trapped in the same sins, and grow older year after year without making any real progress.

In fact, most people have a "pet sin." A pet sin is one that hangs around and attaches itself to you. Instead of shooing it away, like a wild raccoon at your back door, you welcome it with a bowl of milk; and pretty soon that critter becomes rabid and takes up residence in your life. It bites you regularly, but it has become part of your life; and to make it leave would take work. So you make excuses for its behavior and try to keep it hidden because you know others wouldn't think it's a good idea to keep it around. That's a pet sin.

Consider your own life carefully. Do you have a pet sin? Circle anything that you have a hard time controlling:

Eating	**Moodiness**	**Spending**
Sexual Temptation	**Laziness**	**Drinking**
Procrastination	**Temper**	**Gossip**
Pornography	**Criticism**	**Pride**
Bad Language	**Complaining**	**Smoking**

Other: _____

Identifying sins is easy, right? Sins are the things that you know not to do but end up doing anyway. Or they can be the things you know you should do but don't. For instance, you know how to live within a budget, but you overspend anyway. You know the keys required to live a healthy lifestyle, but you choose not to do them. You know talking badly about people is wrong, but you find yourself in gossip once again. This is sin. Paul writes in Romans about this human condition that we all find ourselves struggling with.

Read Romans 7:15, 17-18 in the margin. Write the last three words of verse 18 below:

Is this an excuse? Explain your response.

The last three words of verse 18, *but I can't*, are not meant to be an excuse for us. It's just a fact. Without God's help, we cannot try hard enough or read enough self-help books to overcome the attraction of sin. We need Jesus and the power of the Holy Spirit in our lives to do that. It is through a relationship with Jesus that the Holy Spirit comes to live and work in our lives. It is through His strength that we will have the power to overcome the struggles that are common to us. The key to overcoming sin is the power of God's Spirit at work in our lives.

> **Read Romans 7:24-25; Romans 8:2; and Galatians 5:16 in the margin. What insights do these verses give us regarding the answer to the problem of sin?**

Every fall my driveway is bombarded with maple leaves. At first they are beautiful, but by mid-October the idea of sweeping off the driveway is completely overwhelming. It's practically impossible to do with a broom. So one day I brought home an electric blower. It was like magic. After plugging that tool into the power source, the driveway was clean in a few minutes.

Plugging into God's power through the Holy Spirit works in much the same way. Without the power source, the task is overwhelming. It's just too much to do on our own. But through reading and meditating on God's Word, we open the door to be able to plug into the power source, the Holy Spirit. And through that connection we can do amazing things!

Pray

- Quietly seek God's presence, praising Him for His love and forgiveness.
- Commit today to a daily time of Bible study.
- Be still and ask the Holy Spirit to reveal any areas of sin in your life.
- Repent of these sins and ask for God's strength to overcome patterns or cycles that dishonor Him.

[24]Who will free me from this life that is dominated by sin and death? [25]Thank God! The answer is in Jesus Christ our Lord.
(Romans 7:24-25)

For the new spiritual principle of life "in" Christ lifts me out of the old vicious circle of sin and death.
(Romans 8:2 JBP)

So I say, let the Holy Spirit guide your lives. Then you won't be doing what your sinful nature craves.
(Galatians 5:16)

The key to overcoming sin is the power of God's Spirit at work in our lives.

DAY 5: BUILDING A TEAM

Settle

Set a timer on your phone for two minutes. Just be still and ask the Lord to give you His peace as you focus on Him.

Focus

⁹Two are better off than one, because together they can work more effectively. ¹⁰If one of them falls down, the other can help him up. But if someone is alone and falls, it's just too bad, because there is no one to help him.

(Ecclesiastes 4:9-10 GNT)

¹Then Josiah announced that the Passover of the LORD would be celebrated in Jerusalem, and so the Passover lamb was slaughtered on the fourteenth day of the first month. ²Josiah also assigned the priests to their duties and encouraged them in their work at the Temple of the LORD. ³He issued this order to the Levites, who were to teach all Israel and who had been set apart to serve the LORD: "Put the holy Ark in the Temple that was built by Solomon son of David, the king of Israel. You no longer need to carry it back and forth on your shoulders. Now spend your time serving the LORD your God and his people Israel. ⁴Report for duty according to the family divisions of your ancestors, following the directions of King David of Israel and the directions of his son Solomon.

⁵"Then stand in the sanctuary at the place appointed for your family division and help the families assigned to you as they bring their offerings to the Temple. ⁶Slaughter the Passover lambs, purify yourselves, and prepare to help those who come. Follow all the directions that the LORD gave through Moses."

⁷Then Josiah provided 30,000 lambs and young goats for the people's Passover offerings. . . . ⁸The king's officials also made willing contributions to the people, priests, and Levites. Hilkiah, Zechariah, and Jehiel, the administrators of God's Temple, gave. . . . ⁹The Levite leaders—Conaniah and his brothers Shemaiah and Nethanel, as well as Hashabiah, Jeiel, and Jozabad—gave.

(2 Chronicles 35:1-9)

Reflect

A friend recently asked if I would help her move. I said yes, but let's be honest: does anyone really want to help someone move? Not me, but I love this gal; so I said yes. Moving is hot, sweaty work, and by the end of the day people are usually cranky. I was dreading it. But when the time for the move came, I saw that my friend had brought a team. It wasn't just the two of us. This was going to be a snap. With lots of laughter, new friendships, and a few shared meals, it turned into a good experience. The team made the difference.

There is a beautiful African proverb that says, "If you want to go fast, go alone. If you want to go far, go together." There is great value in building a team if you want real success in life.

Personally, I often like to work alone. There is great satisfaction to me in carving out a few hours of solitude and just knocking stuff out. But I've realized that for the big projects, when something significant needs to happen, I need to be part of a team. Alone I don't have the gifts, stamina, ideas, and time to do all that is required to achieve what God wants to do.

This is true not only in ministry and business but also in our personal lives. This week we are looking at how to grow closer to Christ by examining our lives, identifying destructive patterns, and beginning to get rid of excuses, habits, and sins that keep us from God's best for our lives. One way to increase our chances of living a Christlike life is to build a team. Our odds of success are significantly strengthened when we join with other Christ-followers toward a common goal.

Reread Ecclesiastes 4:9-10 on page 90. According to these verses, what are the benefits of working together?

Recall a time of need in your life when others came to help. How did it affect your relationships?

As we've seen this week, Josiah examined the state of his family, country, and faith and decided to make changes. He moved past excuses and into action. But it's important to note that he did not do this alone. Hilkiah the priest; the prophetess Huldah; Shaphan the secretary; the Levites Jahath, Obadiah, Zechariah; Meshullam; as well as all the elders of Judah and Jerusalem are mentioned as working in harmony with Josiah's goals of restoring God's reign in the kingdom.

As the king, Josiah was in a position to make sweeping reforms, but with the cooperation of others he accomplished more.

Look up the following Scriptures, and note below what each person did to assist King Josiah:

Scripture	Person Named	Contribution
2 Chronicles 34:14		
2 Chronicles 34:16-18		
2 Chronicles 34:22-28		

It was Hilkiah who found the Book of the Law, which had been lost in the temple. (Can you imagine being the one to find the Bible!) It was Shaphan who took it to the king and read it aloud. And it was Huldah the prophetess who instructed Josiah in how God wanted the Scriptures handled. If Shaphan had not brought the Scriptures to Josiah and Huldah had not told him how to handle them, the reforms never would have happened. The contributions of others along with Josiah having the humility and wisdom to receive guidance made the nationwide reform possible. Together these followers of God had greater impact than the king alone could have had.

Another example of the impact of others in Josiah's leadership is shown when he prepared to reinstate the Passover celebration according to the instructions in God's Word. The priests, Levites, and administrators all played an integral role in implementing the restoration of Passover.

Reread 2 Chronicles 35:1-9 (page 90), and note below what role each group played in reinstating the Passover celebration:

The priests:

The Levites:

The administrators:

Josiah did not try to accomplish all of the national reform alone. Wisely, he shared leadership with others and was able to achieve more. They each had a unique role to play. For example, the Levites brought the sacred ark into the temple and made preparations for the sacrifices; the priests oversaw the burnt offerings; the musicians and gatekeepers took on their unique duties; and the officials contributed from their own wealth to make the Passover celebration possible.

Could Josiah have made a difference alone? Yes, probably. But with the partnership of others, his reign was stronger. We read of this principle several places in the Bible. Consider the metaphor of the body in the New Testament:

[14]*For the body does not consist of one member but of many.* [15]*If the foot should say, "Because I am not a hand, I do not belong to the body," that would not make it any less a part of the body.* [16]*And if the ear should say, "Because I am not an eye, I do not belong to the body," that would not make it any less a part of the body.* [17]*If the whole body were an eye, where would be the sense of hearing? If the whole body were an ear, where would be the sense of smell?* [18]*But as it is, God arranged the members in the body, each one of them, as he chose.* [19]*If all were a single member, where would the body be?* [20]*As it is, there are many parts, yet one body.*

[21]*The eye cannot say to the hand, "I have no need of you," nor again the head to the feet, "I have no need of you."* [22]*On the contrary, the parts of the body that seem to be weaker are indispensable,* [23]*and on those parts of the body that we think less honorable we bestow the greater honor, and our unpresentable parts are treated with greater modesty,* [24]*which our more presentable parts do not require. But God has so composed the body, giving greater honor to the part that lacked it,* [25]*that there may be no division in the body, but that the members may have the same care for one another.* [26]*If one member*

suffers, all suffer together; if one member is honored, all rejoice together.

²⁷Now you are the body of Christ and individually members of it.

(1 Corinthians 12:14-27 ESV)

How do these verses support the idea that we each have a unique and important role to play?

You may be familiar with this passage and even have heard sermons preached on it. We are the body of Christ, and like a physical body, we need one another in order to function well. We are healthier and more effective together, especially when we are using our spiritual gifts.

Read the Scriptures below, and list the gifts named in each passage:

Romans 12:6-8

1 Corinthians 12:7-11

Imagine how the strength of your local church would be impacted if each believer in the congregation activated her or his spiritual gifts. I dream of a day when we see gifts such as wisdom, miracles, prophecy, administration, teaching, and exhortation all coming together. What power there is when these gifts are combined! The body is stronger when each part is healthy and functioning as it is intended.

As I write this my husband, Jim, has an injured arm. It has been in a sling for several weeks, and there are things that just have not gotten done around our house recently because I need his strength to do them. As a family, we have missed the use of his right arm. It actually has surprised me how much it has affected us. Can we function? Yes. But we've had to learn to adjust because the "whole" of our family is not in healthy working order right now.

The same is true of the local church. Can we, in our local churches, function without each person taking on their role? Yes. But we do so, metaphorically, with our arms in slings and our legs in casts. It's possible, but it's not as effective as if every member was ready for action.

To learn more about the gifts of the Spirit, read all of Romans 12 and 1 Corinthians 12. If your interest is piqued, then you may want to study and understand what each gift is and look back at times in your life when God has used a particular gift of yours for His purposes. Remember that the spiritual gifts are given to believers in order to build up the church.

Here's something else to keep in mind. Sometimes we simply make being used by God too complicated. I've never met anyone with the spiritual gift of cleaning the bathroom, putting out the parking signs, or folding the programs. But most people I've met do have those abilities. They are physically and mentally able to do the task. Sometimes the problem is not lack of giftedness but lack of willingness.

What spiritual gifts and other unique skills and abilities has God gifted *you* with? If you are not sure, ask family members or friends what gifts they have observed in you.

What are some ways you can use those gifts for God's kingdom? How have you used them in the past in your church or community?

There is strength in doing life together.

Rejoice with those who rejoice, weep with those who weep.
(Romans 12:15 ESV)

A person standing alone can be attacked and defeated, but two can stand back-to-back and conquer. Three are even better, for a triple-braided cord is not easily broken.
(Ecclesiastes 4:12)

When is a time you served outside of your comfort zone? How did it go?

Together, working as a team, we are stronger. In ministry, parenting, friendships, careers, and even small groups, we accomplish more and go further when we work side by side. There is strength in doing life together.

While I was leading a parenting class recently, a young mom of three children under the age of four walked in with a woman I thought must have been her mom or an older friend. As we introduced ourselves, this mom shared that while pregnant with her third child, her husband had been killed in combat. She went to her aunt shortly after that tragedy and said, "I need help raising these kids. Will you help me?" The woman with her was her aunt, who had come alongside her to help with the responsibilities of parenting. This young mom, in the midst of her grief, knew she needed a team.

Read Romans 12:15 and Ecclesiastes 4:12 in the margin. According to these verses, what are some of the reasons for doing life together? What are some of the benefits?

You will face many battles in your lifetime. These battles come in a variety of forms such as sickness, loneliness, discouragement, depression, and even addiction. Whatever form they take, you are more likely to emerge victorious if you are firmly rooted in a relationship with Christ and if you have taken the time to build a team of godly friends around you. Bible studies and ministry teams in the local church are great places to find these friends.

Life is messy, and you are going to need others to help you through hard times and to celebrate with you in the good times. And having a team, as Josiah did, will make it easier for you to accomplish your goals. But these types of relationships rarely happen unless we are intentional in creating them. Having a few people in your life that you can trust on the good days and in your worst moments is a precious gift that will require time, trust, and commitment to develop. You need a few women to whom you can turn for honest feedback, and whom you can trust to give you loving correction when you need it. My friend, you need a God squad, a spiritual posse, who will help you live into your best version of yourself. But choose wisely. Make sure that these are women who love both the Lord and you deeply.

Friends come and friends go, but a true friend sticks by you like family. (Proverbs 18:24 MSG)

Read Proverbs 18:24 and 27:6 in the margin. What do these verses tell us about a true friend?

Wounds from a friend can be trusted, but an enemy multiplies kisses. (Proverbs 27:6 NIV)

Who needs you to have their backs?

Who's already on your spiritual team?

You need a God squad, a spiritual posse, who will help you live into your best version of yourself.

If you don't have a strong team of godly women around you, how could you begin to be intentional about building one?

Our study this week has centered around lessons we can learn from the life of Josiah. He was a young man who broke out of destructive family patterns and moved beyond excuses to lead the people of God faithfully during his lifetime. Second Kings 23:25 gives us a glowing report of his life: "Neither before nor after Josiah was there a king like him who turned to the Lord as he did—with all his heart and with all his soul and with all his strength, in accordance with all the Law of Moses" (NIV).

Like Josiah, may we seek God and follow Him with all our heart, soul, and strength so that we will experience sweet intimacy with the Lord and build lives of beauty and purpose that are pleasing to Him.

Pray

- Thank the Lord for those, by name, who have been part of your spiritual posse.
- If you need to develop your team, then pray and ask God to lead you toward that goal.
- Praise God that you are never alone, that His Spirit is available to you at all times and in all things.

VIDEO VIEWER GUIDE: WEEK 3

Josiah was eight years old when he became king, and he reigned in Jerusalem thirty-one years. He did what was right in the eyes of the LORD and followed the ways of his father David, not turning aside to the right or to the left.

In the eighth year of his reign, while he was still young, he began to seek the God of his father David. In his twelfth year he began to purge Judah and Jerusalem of high places, Asherah poles and idols.

(2 Chronicles 34:1-3 NIV)

Let us examine our ways and test them,
>   and let us return to the LORD.
>   (Lamentations 3:40 NIV)

1. Don't _____.

If you wait for perfect conditions, you will never get anything done.
>   (Ecclesiastes 11:4 TLB)

2. Don't play the _____.

People ruin their lives by their own foolishness
>   and then are angry at the LORD.
>   (Proverbs 19:3)

3. Remove _____.

Do not give the devil a foothold.

  (Ephesians 4:27 NIV)

4. Give God _____.

Looking at them, Jesus said, "With people [as far as it depends on them] it is impossible, but not with God; for all things are possible with God."

      (Mark 10:27 AMP)

Week 4

Mary

Surviving Life's Messy Plot Twists

Luke 1:26-38

DAY 1: BECOMING USABLE

Settle

As you turn aside from today's distractions, consider how God has been at work in your life. Thank Him for His presence in your daily activities.

Focus

"I've told you all this so that trusting me, you will be unshakable and assured, deeply at peace. In this godless world you will continue to experience difficulties. But take heart! I've conquered the world."

(John 16:33 MSG)

26God sent the angel Gabriel to Nazareth, a village in Galilee, 27to a virgin named Mary. She was engaged to be married to a man named Joseph, a descendant of King David. . . .

28Gabriel appeared to her and said, "Greetings, favored woman! The Lord is with you!

29Confused and disturbed, Mary tried to think what the angel could mean. 30"Don't be afraid, Mary," the angel told her, "for you have found favor with God! 31You will conceive and give birth to a son, and you will name him Jesus. 32He will be very great and will be called the Son of the Most High. . . ."

34Mary asked the angel, "But how can this happen? I am a virgin."

35The angel replied, "The Holy Spirit will come upon you, . . . the baby to be born will be holy, and he will be called the Son of God." . . . 37For the word of God will never fail.

38Mary responded, "I am the Lord's servant. May everything you have said about me come true."

(Luke 1:26-32, 34-35, 37-38)

Read Mary's story in Luke 1 and 2.

Reflect

My family loves to go to the movies! We like all types of genres—comedy, action, romance, mystery; but what we really like is when a movie includes a little of all of these. *Princess Bride*, *Star Wars*, and *Guardians of the Galaxy* are movies that we particularly have enjoyed together through the years. Each of these movies has a good story line and a plot twist. We feel warm-hearted about the romance and we laugh at the quirky humor, but what keeps us really engaged is the plot twist. I still remember as a young girl watching when Darth Vader turns to Luke and says, "I am your Father." I did not see that coming!

The twists and turns of the story keep the story line interesting. But when it's our story that takes an unexpected turn, it's not nearly so entertaining—whether good or bad.

When has your life taken an unexpected turn (whether good or bad), and how did you respond initially?

Jim and I were married about six years before we tried to have children. We had been busy with pursuing education and seminary and starting a life together, but children were always part of our dream. When I first suspected I might be pregnant, I secretly bought a home pregnancy test, and—bingo—it was positive. I bought a teddy bear and put a sign around its neck that said, "Congratulations! You're a Daddy!" for Jim to see when he came home. We were thrilled; it was the sweetest time for a few weeks.

On the day of our first sonogram, we couldn't wait to hear the heartbeat and see the child we had begun to call Baby C. But that was a sound we would never hear. As you can imagine, our hearts began to break as we watched the doctor search to find our sweet child's heartbeat without success. I'll never forget the words, "Your child is no longer viable." I wanted to scream, "What? No longer viable—what does that mean? You don't understand; we already love this kid. I bought the bear!"

It felt like I was in an echo chamber as the doctor went on to say, "There is a tumor. . . . We need to do surgery." But all I could really hear was, "Your child is no longer viable."

The next few months were painful. They were hard and we were so very sad. The tumor was removed successfully, but so was a chunk of our hearts.

Our life had taken an unexpected turn. Life felt messy.

When has life dealt you a *crushing* disappointment?

To whom or to what did you turn for help in coping during that time?

Reread John 16:33 (page 103). What does Jesus say that we can expect to experience, and what is the good news He gives us?

> We do not have to lose hope in hard times because we can be unshakable and at peace as we lean into God during those times.

I wish this Scripture said, "In this world you may experience difficulties." But it doesn't. It says "you will." We will experience difficulties in life. Sometimes they are just inconveniences such as having a dead car battery or working late. But other times these difficulties that creep into our lives can disrupt our plans entirely. Cancer, job loss, a betrayal, or an accident are just some examples of life interruptions that can step in and shake our world.

Why do these types of things happen in the first place? Well, in short it's because we live on a broken planet. Our world was created to be perfect; but when sin entered the world, that utopia was shattered. And we must learn to live in the aftermath.

God knows that we live as sinners in a sinful world. He knows that we have difficulties. But John 16:33 promises us that we do not have to lose hope in hard times because we can be unshakable and at peace as we lean into God during those times. This is a powerful promise!

Our Bible study this week is centered around Mary, the mother of Jesus. She is a woman who finds herself confronted with a plot twist early in life—one that will alter the course of her life as well as the lives of everyone who comes to know her son.

Reread Luke 1:28-32 (page 103). Why do you think the angel called Mary a "favored woman"? What might that mean?

There must have been times in her life when Mary felt favored—chosen and special. Here she responded to the angel's amazing news courageously and obediently by saying, essentially, "I am willing to accept whatever God wants." But there must have been other times when she was overwhelmed and scared. Consider what this news would mean for her. Unwed and pregnant, her fiancé surely would at first be confused and disappointed, her child would be born in less than desirable conditions and placed in a manger, and her precious newborn would be hunted by the king. Years later He would be rejected by many and then suffer a painful death on a cross. As those experiences happened, they most likely did not feel like a favored position to Mary.

John 16:33, which we read earlier, had not been written when Mary experienced these trials, but it certainly pertains to her. Life has unexpected twists and difficult circumstances. Mary faced these, and we will too.

Mary's story looks beautiful in stained glass windows. She looks serene in Christmas nativity sets. But in reality her life had many difficulties and often must have seemed very messy. Surely she was ostracized in Nazareth as an unwed teen. What must it have been like to flee to another country to protect her child from King Herod (Matthew 2:13-14)? How did she respond when her other children did not believe Jesus was the Son of God (John 7:5)? And how deeply did her heart break as Jesus was falsely accused, flogged, and then crucified before her eyes (John 19)?

Mary's life was messy, just as our lives are. Yet through it all she was faithful.

Read 1 Peter 4:12-13 in the margin. In light of your current messes or struggles, what comfort do you find in this passage?

¹²Dear friends, don't be surprised at the fiery trials you are going through, as if something strange were happening to you. ¹³Instead, be very glad—for these trials make you partners with Christ in his suffering, so that you will have the wonderful joy of seeing his glory when it is revealed to all the world.

(1 Peter 4:12-13)

Now read Deuteronomy 31:6 and Proverbs 3:5-6 in the margin. As you face hardships, how can you incorporate the truths of these Scriptures into your responses? Write a few practical ideas below:

Mary did not waver in serving God, even when her role became heartbreaking. This week we will look at the qualities in her life that made her usable in messy situations, asking ourselves the question, "Why did God choose Mary to be favored among women?" We will see that she was available, interruptible, trustworthy, and courageous. And we will explore how we, too, can be used by God in mighty ways—even when our lives get messy and do not go as planned.

Pray

- Listen to "Take Courage," recorded by Bethel Music—a powerful ballad about God's presence even when we do not sense His direction.
- Ask God to open your heart this week to discover how you can be fully usable for His purposes.
- Thank God for choosing you as His precious daughter.

"Be strong and courageous. Do not be afraid or terrified…, for the LORD your God goes with you; he will never leave you nor forsake you."
(Deuteronomy 31:6 NIV)

⁵Trust in the LORD with all your heart and lean not on your own understanding; ⁶in all your ways submit to him, and he will make your paths straight.
(Proverbs 3:5-6 NIV)

DAY 2: GOD USES PEOPLE WHO ARE AVAILABLE

Settle

Take the time to sing a song to the Lord, perhaps a favorite hymn or childhood song that brings you comfort.

Focus

And I heard the voice of the Lord saying, "Whom shall I send, and who will go for us?" Then I said, "Here I am! Send me."

(Isaiah 6:8 ESV)

Mary said, "I am the Lord's servant, and I am willing to do whatever he wants. May everything you said come true."

(Luke 1:38 TLB)

Reflect

Early in my life, God and I had a conversation in which I said, "Yes, Sir," to whatever, whenever, and wherever He chose to use me. I don't know how I had the courage to do that. In truth, it probably wasn't courage; it was just the naive prayer of a young girl excited about serving God. I had no idea just what a scary, wonderfully life-altering prayer that would be for me. Essentially, my prayer was saying, "God, use me; I'm available."

This is the essence of the exchange we see between God and Isaiah.

Reread Isaiah 6:8 above. What does Isaiah's response to the Lord reveal about his heart's desire?

Isaiah's desire was to serve God, which requires availability. Being available matters.

For years I have been involved in ministry with students. In fact, I have probably been on about one hundred youth retreats in my lifetime. (There should be a medal for that, by the way!) Early on I stumbled onto what I call a magic bullet. Magic bullets are those great tools that just work and make ministry easier. This one was so easy to implement. During some of our down time while on retreat, I would simply pull away from the crowd of kids and sit alone somewhere out in the open. I didn't take a book or anything with me; I'd just go sit by a lake or find a swing and swing by myself. Without many exceptions, what would happen almost immediately is a sidle. Do you know about sidling? That's when somebody quietly and suddenly comes up beside you. Every time this happened, it was a great opportunity for that student, who wanted to share privately, to have a few moments of one-on-one face time.

Great ministry happens during sidling moments. Once we become available, amazing things happen. Many of the people around us are just looking for someone to be available!

How available or attentive to the needs of others are you throughout your day?

Circle the response that is true most often for you.

Usually Available   Sometimes Available   Rarely Available

This week we are asking the question "Why did God choose Mary?" There are probably many answers to this question but surely one of them is that Mary was available. When the angel came to her and told her news that would forever redirect the course of her life, she didn't argue. She didn't make excuses for why that just wouldn't work well with her schedule. Surely she had many questions, but we see her ask just one.

Read Luke 1:34-35 in the margin. What does Mary want to know?

What answer does the angel give her?

34Mary asked the angel, "But how can I have a baby? I am a virgin."

35The angel replied, "The Holy Spirit shall come upon you, and the power of God shall overshadow you; so the baby born to you will be utterly holy—the Son of God."
(Luke 1:34-35 TLB)

There must have been other questions as well. What will Joseph say? What about my parents? Is there a budget for this? Will I know what to do? Yet we do not see Mary ask any of this. Instead she simply asks how. And the angel gives her a simple and direct answer.

¹³One day some parents brought their children to Jesus so he could lay his hands on them and pray for them. But the disciples scolded the parents for bothering him.

¹⁴But Jesus said, "Let the children come to me. Don't stop them! For the Kingdom of Heaven belongs to those who are like these children."
(Matthew 19:13-14)

————————

¹¹As Jesus continued on toward Jerusalem, he reached the border between Galilee and Samaria. ¹²As he entered a village there, ten men with leprosy stood at a distance, ¹³crying out, "Jesus, Master, have mercy on us!"

¹⁴He looked at them and said, "Go show yourselves to the priests." And as they went, they were cleansed of their leprosy.
(Luke 17:11-14)

Reread Luke 1:38 (page 108). How does Mary's response reveal her availability?

Mary said yes to God, and saying yes to God means being available.

Recall a time when God wanted to use you. Were there any questions you wanted to have answered before you said yes? If so, write them below.

Most of the heroes in the Bible, as well as present-day heroes of the faith, share the trait of being available for God's agenda. Abraham went when God said go, Esther was available at a critical time in history, and Noah built a boat on dry land—all because they were willing to forgo their agenda and follow God's leading.

Jesus was always available for God's agenda. As He interacted with people, He was attentive to their needs.

Read the Scriptures in the margin and note below the specifics of how Jesus is available and present to others in each situation.

Matthew 19:13-14

Luke 17:11-14

Jesus took the time to be with people, to notice them, and to care for their needs. The role of children during Jesus' day was not highly valued, and lepers were literally cast out of mainstream life. Yet Jesus, the great teacher, was available to them. The great miracle worker, God's Son, was not too busy to be available. His schedule had openings, and He took time to be fully present with people.

What are your thoughts as you consider Jesus' example of availability?

How available are *you* when it comes to hearing and responding to God's voice?

Would you be willing to tell God in advance that you are available to be used by Him? Explain your response.

Most of the heroes in the Bible share the trait of being available for God's agenda.

One of my favorite long-time Christian artists is Steven Curtis Chapman. His music has been a constant source of hope to me for decades. Years ago I heard him sing "I Will Be Here," a song he wrote to his wife. Throughout the song he describes times and ways that uncertainty and fear might come, always responding with the promise, "I will be here." It is beautifully touching as a song of marriage; but often when I hear it, I consider it as God's message to me. Whatever happens, God is always here—always with me.

Just as God is always available to us as our Father, Friend, and Savior, we have the opportunity to be available to Him. Mary was available, and as a result she played an integral role in the redemption story of the human race. God has a role for you to play also. Are you available?

Pray

- Search online for the song and/or lyrics to "I Will Be Here," and consider the words as an expression of God's deep love and availability for you.

- I want to invite you to pray the same prayer that I prayed as a teenager. In fact, if possible, kneel wherever you are right now and pray something like this:

God, in advance I say yes. Yes, use me—however, whenever, and wherever you choose. Interrupt my plans for Yours. I invite You to use me to achieve Your will in me and through me. Help me to trust You and have the courage to be available. I love You and want to give myself wholly to You. Amen.

Congratulations! If you just prayed that prayer for the first time, buckle up! You are in for an exciting and rewarding ride, because availability is a key to partnering with God to do amazing things!

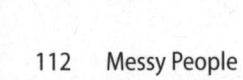

DAY 3: GOD USES PEOPLE WHO ARE INTERRUPTIBLE

Settle

Put aside the mental to-do list for a moment and be still. Once your heart is settled, pray Psalm 103:1-4 to God:

¹Let all that I am praise the LORD;
   with my whole heart, I will praise his holy name.
²Let all that I am praise the LORD;
   may I never forget the good things he does for me.
³He forgives all my sins
   and heals all my diseases.
⁴He redeems me from death
   and crowns me with love and tender mercies.

Focus

However, as it is written:

"What no eye has seen,
      what no ear has heard,
and what no human mind has conceived"—
      the things God has prepared for those who love him.

(1 Corinthians 2:9 NIV)

¹At that time the Roman emperor, Augustus, decreed that a census should be taken throughout the Roman Empire.... ⁴And because Joseph was a descendant of King David, he had to go to Bethlehem in Judea.... ⁵He took with him Mary, to whom he was engaged, who was now expecting a child.

⁶And while they were there, the time came for her baby to be born. ⁷She gave birth to her firstborn son. She wrapped him snugly in strips of cloth and laid him in a manger, because there was no lodging available for them.

(Luke 2:1, 4-7)

Reflect

When I was in the seventh grade, I pictured my middle school as a prison. The teachers were the guards, the principal was the warden, and I, of course, was one of the inmates. I vividly remember looking out the window of my social studies class, watching cars go by, and thinking, *One day I will be free! Free to go to lunch when I want to without standing in a straight line. Free to choose a job. Free to drive around. No more problems and nobody telling me what to do all day long.*

I had a seventh-grade ideal picture of my future perfect life. This included my husband, the dentist—not doctor, because I didn't want him to have to take too many late-night calls; my three adoring and beautiful children, all two years apart in age; and my successful executive position where I worked ten hours a week (no, not ten hours a day, but ten hours a week; I didn't want to be too stressed out!).

So in college, when I began to fall head-over-heels for a guy that my friends called the "Captain of the God-Squad," I thought, *Oh, wait a minute, God! This was not the plan!* I had encountered a major plot twist! My story was not developing as I had envisioned. The great news, which I quickly realized, was that God had a much better plan in mind for my life.

Now, it's not wrong to plan. In fact, setting godly goals and going after them is admirable. But we can't let our goals become the goal. We have to be willing to let our agenda be interruptible if we want to receive God's best in our lives.

In the prayer that He taught His disciples, Jesus models for us how we should pray and, to some degree, how we should set goals. He doesn't say "My will be done" but "Thy will be done" (Matthew 6:10 KJV). Replacing our will with God's will and remaining interruptible is part of the secret to being used in miraculous ways in this life!

What plans have you made for yourself that God has replaced with better ones?

How has praying for God's will to be done blessed you? Recall a specific situation if you can.

Has pursuing your will versus God's will ever caused you to stumble? If so, explain briefly.

Saying yes to God means being interruptible.

Personally, I've found that some of my sweetest moments in life are when I am interrupted. Recently I was rushing around after a worship service when a young woman came up to me and said, "I see you're busy, but do you have a moment?" In truth, I *was* busy. In fact, I was late to a meeting, and I hate to be late. But she continued by saying, "Would you hold my baby and pray for her? I'm struggling in my faith right now, and I'd like someone who isn't struggling to love on her a moment. She deserves that." It was the sweetest, purest moment I had experienced in a long time. What a privilege it was for me to pray over both this mother and her baby.

Saying yes to God means being interruptible.

When your plans are interrupted, how do you usually feel?

How interruptible is your schedule right now?

Can you recall a specific time when you said yes to God by allowing yourself to be interrupted? If so, describe it briefly:

I wonder if young Mary ever looked out the window, as I did as a teenager, dreaming of the future. Surely she too had dreams of what her life would look like—perhaps dreams of a husband and children and the work she might do. But God threw her a very significant plot twist early in life. Her plans were interrupted, and this interruption was complicated. Even so, God could see the big picture, and Mary trusted in that. As a result of that trust, she played an integral role in raising the Son of God! She had the privilege of partnering with God to do something beyond anything she possibly could have dreamed of on her own.

Mary is a great example of someone who was interruptible, and so is her son. Throughout Jesus' ministry, He was constantly interrupted. There were parents wanting Him to bless their children (Luke 18:15-17); disciples constantly asking questions (Luke 8:9); people pressing in, hoping for a miracle (Mark 5:25-34); and even those who would break in through a roof in order to help their friend (Luke 5:17-39).

When people sought Jesus, He was not only available; He was interruptible. He didn't scold people for wanting to get close to Him. He was patient with the children. He didn't complain when the roof was torn apart. And He didn't fuss when the woman touched the hem of His robe for healing. He was available and interruptible.

How might your life be enriched if you determined to always be interruptible?

Read 1 Corinthians 2:9 (see below). How would you describe or explain what is implied by this verse?

As I studied this verse, the first few words jumped out at me: "as it is written...." The apostle Paul goes on to quote a passage from the Old Testament:

> *"What no eye has seen,*
> *what no ear has heard,*
> *and what no human mind has conceived"*—
> *the things God has prepared for those who love him.*
> (1 Corinthians 2:9 NIV)

I looked up the cross-reference in my Bible to discover where and to whom this was originally written, and I discovered that it comes from Isaiah 64:4. This is interesting because Isaiah, who was the key character of our study yesterday, is the one who said to God, "Here I am! Send me" (Isaiah 6:8 ESV). He was available and interruptible. And now here toward the end

of Isaiah's book, we see the promise of God to him. God basically tells him, "Isaiah, you can't see or hear or even dream up what I have prepared for your life!"

I want to live believing that is true in my life, don't you?

Isaiah was interruptible. He surrendered his agenda to God's will. Jesus did the same. In Luke chapter 8 we see Jesus pressed by the crowds, yet at the touch from a woman in need, He altered his day to care for her.

[40]On the other side of the lake the crowds welcomed Jesus, because they had been waiting for him. [41]Then a man named Jairus, a leader of the local synagogue, came and fell at Jesus' feet, pleading with him to come home with him. [42]His only daughter, who was about twelve years old, was dying.

As Jesus went with him, he was surrounded by the crowds. [43]A woman in the crowd had suffered for twelve years with constant bleeding, and she could find no cure. [44]Coming up behind Jesus, she touched the fringe of his robe. Immediately, the bleeding stopped.

[45]"Who touched me?" Jesus asked.

Everyone denied it, and Peter said, "Master, this whole crowd is pressing up against you."

[46]But Jesus said, "Someone deliberately touched me, for I felt healing power go out from me." [47]When the woman realized that she could not stay hidden, she began to tremble and fell to her knees in front of him. The whole crowd heard her explain why she had touched him and that she had been immediately healed. [48]"Daughter," he said to her, "your faith has made you well. Go in peace."

(Luke 8:40-48)

In this story, Jesus is on His way to the home of Jairus whose daughter is on the edge of death. Imagine how frustrated Jairus must be when Jesus is interrupted! In fact, by the time Jesus reaches the home, the little girl has passed away. But God's plans are bigger than what we can see. Jesus takes the time to be fully present with the bleeding woman who touches His robe, and this delay makes it possible for Him to do the tremendous miracle of raising a little girl from death to life. Rather than simply healing the sick, He raises the dead!

I want to be available and interruptible like Mary and Jesus. But if I'm entirely truthful, I have to admit that sometimes interruptions aggravate me.

They put me behind schedule, which means I don't get to everything on my to-do list. Sometimes I am even asked to give up things that I want in order to do the things I sense that God or others want. And that can be frustrating. But it's worth it, because so often in those moments of interruption we have Holy Opportunities.

If I could go back and talk to my seventh-grade self, I would tell that kiddo, "Relax, this season won't last long. God has great things for you. Just keep running toward Him, and He'll reveal the rest to you at just the right time."

We all face plot twists and life interruptions. Mary did, and we surely will as well. Surrendering to God and staying alert for His direction can give you a new sense of peace and adventure.

Pray

- Pray the Lord's prayer line by line, adapting this familiar passage into your own words.

Example:
Our Father which art in heaven, Hallowed be thy name . . .
Sweet Heavenly Father, precious and holy and sacred are You!

[9]*Our Father which art in heaven, Hallowed be thy name.*

[10]*Thy kingdom come, Thy will be done in earth, as it is in heaven.*

[11]*Give us this day our daily bread.*

[12]*And forgive us our debts, as we forgive our debtors.*

[13]*And lead us not into temptation, but deliver us from evil: For thine is the kingdom, and the power, and the glory, for ever. Amen.*

(Matthew 6:9-13 KJV)

Ask God to give you a heart that is interruptible and that yearns for His will to be done in your life.

DAY 4: GOD USES PEOPLE WHO ARE TRUSTWORTHY

Settle

"Trust and obey, for there's no other way to be happy in Jesus, but to trust and obey."[1] Take a few minutes to reflect on these lines from an old hymn, and allow the simplicity of the message to calm you.

Focus

For the eyes of the LORD run to and fro throughout the whole earth, to show Himself strong on behalf of those whose heart is loyal to Him.

(2 Chronicles 16:9 NKJV)

[46]And Mary said:

> "My soul glorifies the Lord
> > [47]and my spirit rejoices in God my Savior,
> [48]for he has been mindful
> > of the humble state of his servant.
> From now on all generations will call me blessed,
> > [49]for the Mighty One has done great things for me—
> > holy is his name.
> [50]His mercy extends to those who fear him,
> > from generation to generation.
> [51]He has performed mighty deeds with his arm;
> > he has scattered those who are proud in their inmost thoughts.
> [52]He has brought down rulers from their thrones
> > but has lifted up the humble.
> [53]He has filled the hungry with good things
> > but has sent the rich away empty.
> [54]He has helped his servant Israel,
> > remembering to be merciful
> [55]to Abraham and his descendants forever,
> > just as he promised our ancestors."

(Luke 1:46-55 NIV)

Reflect

When our daughter, Alyssa, was born, it was miraculous and wonderful and all the sweet things that bringing a child into the world should be. But thirty-six hours later, a nurse came into my hospital room, handed us our newborn, and told us that it was time for us to head home. It was one of the most terrifying moments of my entire life!

What was this woman thinking?

We had not raised a child before. I actually asked the nurse, "Are you entrusting her care to us? What if we screw her up?" My husband and I could not believe that the life of another human being now rested in our hands.

In those first few months as a parent, a friend gave me some great advice. She said, "Just guide this child with the big picture in mind. Imagine her at thirty years old. What do you want her to be like? What is her character? Now chip away everything that doesn't reflect that." That advice resonated with me; and as Alyssa grew, it helped me to not be discouraged by the small things and to focus on God's bigger picture for her life.

We had prayed for this child. God had blessed us with her, and we wanted to be found faithful in how we raised her. In a world where it is easy to become distracted with busyness, we were committed to focusing on what mattered most. And more than anything else, we wanted Alyssa to know Christ as her Savior and serve Him with her whole heart. God was trusting us to stay close to Him and allow Him to lead us in this new role. It was another opportunity for us to be faithful.

As I think about Mary, most favored among women, I realize God was trusting her in much the same way. I don't know a lot of details about Mary, but I am confident of this: long before she was pregnant with Jesus, she said, "Yes, God, I am available and interruptible; and I can be trusted with Your will for my life."

Saying yes to God means being trustworthy.

When has God trusted you with a task that seemed much too large for you?

What gifts (people, resources, and abilities) has God entrusted to you?

Saying yes to God means being trustworthy.

As we saw earlier this week, after being greeted by a celestial angel and hearing the unexpected proclamation that she, an unmarried virgin, was destined to conceive and bear God's Son, Mary responded with these beautiful words: "I am the Lord's servant. . . . May your word to me be fulfilled" (Luke 1:38 NIV).

What an awesome example of what trust in God looks like. Even when Mary didn't understand all that this pregnancy would mean, she trusted God and was available to be used by Him.

Soon after receiving her life-changing news, Mary left for Judea to be with her cousin, Elizabeth. It was shortly after Mary's arrival there that she sang a song of praise to God for who He is and how He was blessing her. This song is even more evidence of the character of trust between Mary and her heavenly Father.

Reread Luke 1:46-48 (page 119). What evidence of Mary's trust do you find in these verses? What has God done for her?

Now reread 2 Chronicles 16:9 (page 119). According to this verse, what will God do for those who faithfully trust Him?

Do you tend to trust God even when you don't fully understand His plan? Why or why not?

Near the cross of
Jesus stood his
mother.

(John 19:25 NIV)

The Great Commandment

³⁶*"Teacher, which
is the greatest
commandment in
the Law?"*

³⁷*Jesus replied:
"'Love the Lord
your God with all
your heart and
with all your soul
and with all your
mind.'* ³⁸*This is the
first and greatest
commandment.*
³⁹*And the second
is like it: 'Love
your neighbor
as yourself.'* ⁴⁰*All
the Law and the
Prophets hang
on these two
commandments."*

*(Matthew
22:36-40 NIV)*

Think about Mary's situation. She didn't just have a baby. She raised God's Son. She nursed Him and cared for Him. She played with Him and taught Him. She served Him and wept over Him.

Read John 19:25 in the margin, and let these words sink in. What must that experience have been like for Mary? What must she have been feeling? How would you have felt in her place?

Mary wasn't only there for the birthday parties and the awards days at school—or whatever the ordinary, everyday experiences of Jesus' life were. She was there when others fled. She was there in the good times as well as in the bad times that surely must have crushed her heart. Why?

Because, like most mothers, she loved her son. But I believe it also was because she loved God. She had been entrusted with the responsibility of Jesus' care, and she was not going to let God down. Mary was trustworthy with the task that God had put before her.

What task or responsibility has God put before you?

Regardless of the specific tasks that each of us has been given, all of us who follow Jesus have been entrusted with a sacred mission. This mission is well defined through two key verses given to us by Jesus Himself.

Read Matthew 22:36-40 (in the margin)and Matthew 28:18-20 (in the margin of page 123) , and write these two vital commands of Christ in your own words below:

The Great Commandment:

The Great Commission:

As those who believe in and follow Jesus, we also have been entrusted with specific gifts and abilities.

Read 1 Peter 4:10 in the margin. For what purpose have we been given these gifts? How are we to use them?

Notice that this verse tells us we should use whatever gifts are at our disposal—meaning spiritual gifts, abilities, talents, and resources—to serve others. It does not say we are to use them to make money or bring glory to ourselves but to serve others. This is how we faithfully steward or manage God's grace given to us.

At the end of Week 3, we looked briefly at spiritual gifts. Review the gifts you listed and the ways you've used them in your church or community (page 95). What are some specific ways you have used all of the gifts at your disposal—spiritual gifts, abilities, talents, and resources—to help others? Describe a few examples below.

Reread 2 Chronicles 16:9 (page 119). According to this verse, what kind of people is God looking for, and what does He promise to do for them?

The Great Commission

[18]*"All authority in heaven and on earth has been given to me.* [19]*Therefore go and make disciples of all nations, baptizing them in the name of the Father and of the Son and of the Holy Spirit,* [20]*and teaching them to obey everything I have commanded you. And surely I am with you always, to the very end of the age."*

(Matthew 28:18-20 NIV)

———————

Each of you should use whatever gift you have received to serve others, as faithful stewards of God's grace in its various forms.

(1 Peter 4:10 NIV)

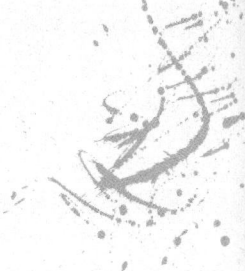

The image of God scanning the planet looking for someone who is ready to move into action is powerful. So far this week we have seen that God is looking for people who are available, interruptible, and trustworthy. When we turn our hearts fully toward Him as laborers in God's fields, miraculous results are produced!

Pray

- Express gratitude to God for the opportunity to partner with Him in life, thanking Him that you don't have to face anything alone.
- Ask Him for strength when you find it difficult to trust Him.
- Praise Him for the blessings He has given you and those you have yet to receive.

DAY 5: GOD USES PEOPLE WHO ARE COURAGEOUS

Settle

Fear can rob us of peace. As you take time to slow your thoughts today, ask God to drive out all worry and fear and give you peace so that you may focus on Him alone in these next moments.

Focus

"The LORD himself goes before you and will be with you; he will never leave you nor forsake you. Do not be afraid; do not be discouraged."

(Deuteronomy 31:8 NIV)

[26]In the sixth month of Elizabeth's pregnancy, God sent the angel Gabriel to Nazareth, a town in Galilee, [27]to a virgin pledged to be married to a man named Joseph, a descendant of David. The virgin's name was Mary. [28]The angel went to her and said, "Greetings, you who are highly favored! The Lord is with you."

[29]Mary was greatly troubled at his words and wondered what kind of greeting this might be. [30]But the angel said to her, "Do not be afraid, Mary; you have found favor with God."

(Luke 1:26-30 NIV)

Reflect

My husband, Jim, is a cowboy wanna-be. He loves horses, rounding up cattle, and adventure. His perfect day off leaves him sweaty and smelling of the barn. In fact, my son's friends call him the Cowboy Pastor. So, it's not surprising that he often quotes not only Scripture but also John Wayne movies. One of his favorite John Wayne sayings is, "Courage is being scared to death but saddling up anyway."[2]

Fear must have been a daily companion of the Old Testament prophets and heroes. Moses, Joshua, Daniel, Jeremiah, Isaiah, and Elisha all spoke against the cultural influences of surrounding nations as they spoke for the Lord. Surely they must have been frightened often as they followed God's leading. For example, we know that Joshua faced fear as he stepped into

Saying yes to God means being courageous.

the role of Moses' successor—a role in which he would lead the people to defeat their enemies in the Promised Land.

Reread Deuteronomy 31:8 on page 125. How do we know from this verse that Joshua is afraid? What does Moses tell him?

Despite fear, Joshua saddled up anyway—as did other biblical heroes. If we are to be used by God, we too will need large doses of courage to counteract the fear that will accompany stepping out in faith. Saying yes to God means being courageous.

If you are to be available, interruptible, and trustworthy so that you can say yes to God, then you are going to need courage—because moving from your will into God's will can be a scary, overwhelming endeavor. It will move you outside your comfort zone, requiring you to move in faith against the fears that are holding you back.

What fears have kept you from being used by God in the past?

What fears do you continue to confront?

Let's consider some of the fears Mary must have faced by looking again to some verses we explored earlier in the week.

Reread Luke 1:26-30 (page 125). What was Mary's reaction to the angel's news in verse 29? What words would you use to describe her at this point in the story?

When Mary was first visited by the angel, we see that she was confused and disturbed by the encounter. In other words, Mary was afraid. She must have been asking herself, "What is happening here?" Thankfully, her fears were addressed directly by the angel. The Living Bible says it this way: "Don't be frightened, Mary…God has decided to wonderfully bless you!" (Luke 1:30, emphasis added).

The angel's news continues in the next verses.

Read Luke 1:31-32 in the margin. According to these verses, how was God going to bless Mary?

31"You will conceive and give birth to a son, and you are to call him Jesus. 32He will be great and will be called the Son of the Most High."

(Luke 1:31-32 NIV)

As we saw on Day 2, Mary did not argue with the angel but simply asked one clarifying question: "How will this be…since I am a virgin?" (Luke 1:34 NIV). She wasn't argumentative. She didn't negotiate. She was just curious about the logistics. In other words, "This is not how my mom told me things would happen."

Mary received her answer, but it must have left her a bit confused also: "The angel answered, 'The Holy Spirit will come on you, and the power of the Most High will overshadow you'" (Luke 1:35 NIV). Surely she must have wondered, *Overshadow me? What does that mean? I've never heard of that before.*

Then there must have been the fear of how her parents would react. The Bible doesn't tell us how it went with her mom and dad, but certainly they must have been skeptical of her story. Perhaps they were angry or disappointed, wondering if she was lying. Though we can't know for sure, I wonder if that was why Mary hurried off to her cousin Elizabeth's home in Judea. Did her family want to keep her out of public view and away from the gossips of Nazareth?

As we've seen, despite all of the fears of what others might think and what this might mean for her future, Mary responded in faith and with courage.

Read Luke 1:38 in the margin, and rewrite Mary's response in your own words—as you might say it:

"I am the Lord's servant," Mary answered. "May your word to me be fulfilled."

(Luke 1:38 NIV)

Now, let's consider Mary's fiancé, Joseph. Did his heart break upon hearing that Mary was pregnant, knowing the child could not possibly be his? What fears must he have faced?

18This is how the birth of Jesus the Messiah came about: His mother Mary was pledged to be married to Joseph, but before they came together, she was found to be pregnant through the Holy Spirit. 19Because Joseph her husband was faithful to the law, and yet did not want to expose her to public disgrace, he had in mind to divorce her quietly.

(Matthew 1:18-19 NIV)

Read Matthew 1:18–19 in the margin. What clues do we find in verse 19 regarding Joseph's response?

Joseph wanted to do the right thing in an embarrassing situation. By law, he could have had Mary killed for infidelity, but that's not what he wanted. He appears to have just wanted distance. So a quiet divorce must have seemed to be his only option—until God sent an angel to him also.

Read Matthew 1:20-21 in the margin. What similarities do you see between the angel's message to Joseph and the angel's message to Mary, which we read earlier?

Notice the words "Do not be afraid." Joseph, like Mary, was encouraged to overcome fear—to be courageous and live out God's plan! But there were obstacles he would have to face as well. What would his parents have to say about this? What about the other people in the village?

God spoke to Joseph through an angel in a dream and relieved some of his fears, but it was still up to Joseph to act. He also had to be available, interruptible, trustworthy, and courageous. Not only do Mary and Joseph share these traits, but most other biblical heroes do as well—heroes such as Moses, Abraham, Noah, Deborah, Peter, and Paul.

20"Joseph son of David, do not be afraid to take Mary home as your wife, because what is conceived in her is from the Holy Spirit. 21She will give birth to a son, and you are to give him the name Jesus, because he will save his people from their sins."

(Matthew 1:20-21 NIV)

Where are you currently in regards to the four attributes we've studied this week? For each attribute, put a check mark in the appropriate column:

Attribute	This Is Me	Somewhat	Not Much	Nope, Not At All
Available				
Interruptible				
Trustworthy				
Courageous				

If you knew that you had nothing to be afraid of, what would you attempt today for God?

It's important to acknowledge that even when we are available, interruptible, trustworthy, and courageous—even when we are following God's plan—life can still be messy. Faithful people encounter messy situations. Mary certainly did. Her role in God's plan brought both joy and sadness and must have seemed messy at times. Yet it was because she was available, interruptible, trustworthy, and courageous that she was able to partner with God in the greatest rescue mission of all time! God wants to partner with you too. Incorporating this week's values will help you be ready when God presents those opportunities.

Pray

- Listen to "Oh My Soul," recorded by Casting Crowns, or another song about trusting God through difficult or unexpected circumstances.
- Thank God for how He has been present in your life through the messy plot twists of life.
- Ask God again for courage to be used for His great purposes in your life.

"Here on earth you will have many trials and sorrows. But take heart, because I have overcome the world."

(John 16:33 NLT)

Instead of being shocked and surprised when life abruptly brings us a plot twist, we have to _____ in advance: How will I _____ when the plot twist comes my way?

If you want to make a difference . . . it begins with you. It begins with having the _____ to step out—to think and act in _____ _____.

Do not conform to the pattern of this world, but be transformed by the renewing of your mind.

(Romans 12:2 NIV)

When the Lord God saw the extent of human wickedness, and that the trend and direction of men's lives were only towards evil, he was sorry he had made them. It broke his heart. . . . But Noah was a pleasure to the Lord.

(Genesis 6:5-6, 8 TLB)

Noah did all that the Lord commanded him.

(Genesis 7:5 NIV)

What do you see in your world that needs to be _____? What has God been wanting to _____ with you to do?

Week 5

David

Overcoming the Mess of Criticism

1 Samuel 16–18;
2 Samuel 12; 15

DAY 1: RESPONDING TO CRITICISM

Settle

As you quiet your heart before God today, pray back to Him Psalm 23, written by King David.

¹The LORD is my shepherd; I shall not want.

²He maketh me to lie down in green pastures: he leadeth me beside the still waters.

³He restoreth my soul: he leadeth me in the paths of righteousness for his name's sake.

⁴Yea, though I walk through the valley of the shadow of death, I will fear no evil: for thou art with me; thy rod and thy staff they comfort me.

⁵Thou preparest a table before me in the presence of mine enemies: thou anointest my head with oil; my cup runneth over.

⁶Surely goodness and mercy shall follow me all the days of my life: and I will dwell in the house of the LORD for ever.

(KJV)

Focus

⁵I depend on God alone;
    I put my hope in him.
⁶He alone protects and saves me;
    he is my defender,
    and I shall never be defeated.
⁷My salvation and honor depend on God;
    he is my strong protector;
    he is my shelter.

(Psalm 62:5-7 GNT)

²⁸But when David's oldest brother, Eliab, heard David talking to the men, he was angry. "What are you doing here anyway?" he demanded. "What about those few sheep you're supposed to be taking care of? I know about your pride and deceit. You just want to see the battle!"

²⁹"What have I done now?" David replied. "I was only asking a question!'"

(1 Samuel 17:28-29)

Reading David's Story (optional): In 1 and 2 Samuel there are forty chapters dedicated to telling the story of David's triumphs and tragedies (1 Samuel 16–2 Samuel 24). If you have the time and are up for the challenge, you can read eight chapters each day of our study this week and finish by the end of the week! Today, read 1 Samuel 16–23.

Reflect

This week we have been diving into the tough topic of criticism. Let's face it, criticism is hard. It often comes at us from many different angles; and if we don't learn to deal with it wisely, we can find ourselves discouraged and frazzled as we see in the following fable.

A Man and his son were once going with their Donkey to market. As they were walking along by its side a countryman passed them and said: "You fools, what is a Donkey for but to ride upon?"

So the Man put the Boy on the Donkey and they went on their way. But soon they passed a group of men, one of whom said: "See that lazy youngster, he lets his father walk while he rides."

So the Man ordered his Boy to get off, and got on himself. But they hadn't gone far when they passed two women, one of whom said to the other: "Shame on that lazy lout to let his poor little son trudge along."

Well, the Man didn't know what to do, but at last he took his Boy up before him on the Donkey. By this time they had come to the town, and the passers-by began to jeer and point at them. The Man stopped and asked what they were scoffing at. The men said: "Aren't you ashamed of yourself for overloading that poor donkey with you and your hulking son?"

The Man and Boy got off and tried to think what to do. They thought and they thought, till at last they cut down a pole, tied the donkey's feet to it, and raised the pole and the donkey to their shoulders. They went along amid the laughter of all who met them till they came to Market Bridge, when the Donkey, getting one of his feet loose, kicked out and caused the Boy to drop his end of the pole. In the struggle the Donkey fell over the bridge, and his fore-feet being tied together he was drowned.

"That will teach you," said an old man who had followed them:

"Please all, and you will please none."[1]

It's true: You simply cannot please everyone. There are always going to be people in your life who criticize you and speak against you. It's inevitable. You will be misunderstood, misquoted, unfairly judged, attacked, and gossiped about. It's part of life on planet earth. If you are swayed by every opinion like the father in the fable, you will not live a very fruitful life. You cannot allow every criticism to determine how you will live. But this is easier said than done, right?

When was the last time you were criticized, attacked, or judged? Briefly describe the situation and how it made you feel.

I hate to be misunderstood, misrepresented, and gossiped about. But it happens. And when it does, I usually have several reactions. It's like different parts of me want to take over and handle it:

My mouth wants to defend and set the record straight.
My heart just hurts and wants to find healing.
My mind seeks to understand if it is truth or jealousy.
My soul wants to hug the person and restore the relationship.
My feet want to run away and quit putting myself out there for others to judge.
And, if I'm honest, sometimes my hand wants to slap the person against the side of the head!

Criticism hurts. No matter how many positives we have in our lives, one phone call, letter, e-mail, or conversation can turn us inside out. Especially if the criticism comes from someone we trust or someone who is close to us. These wounds may leave our hearts broken and our minds wondering why we even allow people to get close to us.

Criticism hurts, and how we process it is important.

I remember vividly a time when I was a little girl and an older relative told me that I had pretty eyes but my cousin was the pretty one. I didn't lash out or defend myself; I just accepted those words as my truth. They weren't spoken to encourage me; they hurt. And because I didn't have the tools at eight years old to process that criticism, I allowed them to shape my view of myself. I was not the pretty one. In fact, when I was honored in college by being elected to homecoming court, my first response was that this must be a campus-wide joke to embarrass me.

It was thirty years later—thirty years—that I looked into a mirror and finally told that little girl that she was beautiful.

Criticism hurts, and how we process it is important. I tend to allow a critical comment to wound and discourage me, but you may have a more direct response. When attacked, you may want to attack back. When insulted, you may want to retaliate. These may be natural responses; but like my internal pity party, they're not helpful.

How has past criticism affected you over time?

How do you typically respond when criticized?

Ideally, what would you like your response to be when criticized?

This week we're going to look at the life of David—a shepherd, king, warrior, husband, and father who was criticized and attacked much of his life. In fact, throughout the years there were people who spoke badly of him and wanted to kill him. Yet the Bible describes David as a man after God's own heart (Acts 13:22). If this man who loved God so passionately and served God so faithfully was criticized, then we can know that we will have to deal with criticism too.

In a sense, a form of criticism began when David was young. God sent the prophet Samuel to Bethlehem to find a man named Jesse and anoint one of his sons to replace Saul as the next king of Israel (1 Samuel 16:1), and Jesse did not bother to call David in from the fields. Apparently, as the youngest of Jesse's sons, David was not even a serious consideration as someone to be used by God. We find the story in 1 Samuel 16.

Read 1 Samuel 16:1-12. How do you imagine young David might have felt in this situation?

According to verse 7, what mattered to God in choosing the next king?

One chapter later, in 1 Samuel 17, we see David criticized openly by his oldest brother, other soldiers, and King Saul when he steps forward with the courage to challenge Goliath.

Read 1 Samuel 17:28-37. What kind of criticism did David face on this occasion, and what was his response?

Despite repeated criticism, David persisted in wanting to defend Israel's honor by fighting Goliath—which he eventually did.

Read 1 Samuel 17:41-44. Why did Goliath despise David, and how did he taunt him?

⁵I depend on
God alone;
   I put my hope
   in him.
⁶He alone protects
and saves me;
   he is my defender,
   and I shall never
   be defeated.
⁷My salvation and
honor depend
on God;
   he is my strong
   protector;
   he is my shelter.
   (Psalm 62:5-7 GNT)

Now read 1 Samuel 17:45-47. How would you summarize David's response?

So as a teenager David had to learn to deal with critics, which he did by trusting and relying on God. From then on, critics would be his constant companion throughout his life. Among his many detractors were his brother, king, wife, son, and at one point, even his trusted advisor. Their criticism stemmed from a variety of sources including jealousy, embarrassment, greed, and even truth. David had many occasions when he had to ignore and move past his critics, as he did when his wife mocked his worship and when his brother questioned his motives. Then there were times when David needed to stop, listen, and repent, as he did in response to Nathan's rebuke after his sins of adultery and murder. There also were times when David had to confront the criticism, such as with his own son Absalom who sought to take the kingdom from him.

Through it all, David always turned to God for strength and truth, as he reveals in the many psalms that he wrote, such as:

You, God, are my God,
   earnestly I seek you;
I thirst for you,
   my whole being longs for you.
      (Psalm 63:1 NIV)

⁴Show me your ways, LORD,
   teach me your paths.
⁵Guide me in your truth and teach me,
   for you are God my Savior,
   and my hope is in you all day long.
      (Psalm 25:4-5 NIV)

Read Psalm 62:5-7 in the margin. How does David describe God in these verses?

Like David, we are going to encounter criticism. Throughout life people will want to attack us for many different reasons. But also like David, we can let God be our protector, our Savior, our defender, our guide, and our shelter. Call out to your heavenly Father, just as David did, when you feel attacked. Be raw and authentic, knowing that God loves you and wants to protect you in your times of distress.

Pray

- Listen to "Your Love Defends Me," recorded by Matt Maher.
- Thank God for being your biggest fan and defender.
- Ask God for His peace to face the critics of your life.
- Pray for insight into how to handle criticism in a way that honors Christ.

DAY 2: IMITATING CHRIST

Settle

Stand and take a deep breath in, raising your hands above your head. Hold that breath five seconds, and then slowly exhale. As you exhale, allow the troubles of the day to leave you. Do it several times if you need to exhale a lot of troubles!

Focus

A *gentle answer turns away wrath,*
> *but a harsh word stirs up anger.*
> (Proverbs 15:1 NIV)

¹*After Saul returned from pursuing the Philistines, he was told, "David is in the Desert of En Gedi." ²So Saul took three thousand able young men from all Israel and set out to look for David and his men near the Crags of the Wild Goats.*

³*He came to the sheep pens along the way; a cave was there, and Saul went in to relieve himself. David and his men were far back in the cave. ⁴The men said, "This is the day the LORD spoke of when he said to you, 'I will give your enemy into your hands for you to deal with as you wish.' " Then David crept up unnoticed and cut off a corner of Saul's robe.*

⁵*Afterward, David was conscience-stricken for having cut off a corner of his robe. ⁶He said to his men, "The LORD forbid that I should do such a thing to my master, the LORD's anointed, or lay my hand on him; for he is the anointed of the LORD." ⁷With these words David sharply rebuked his men and did not allow them to attack Saul. And Saul left the cave and went his way.*

> (1 Samuel 24:1-7 NIV)

Reading David's Story (optional): Read 1 Samuel 24–31.

Reflect

My husband, Jim, and I don't argue that often; but when we do, it's intense. We are both driven, strong people; so when we disagree, there's the potential for fireworks. It's real July 4th kind of stuff. But I discovered a secret years ago that has diffused things between us dozens of times in the past. It just may work for you too. Are you ready for it? Here it is. When the tension is thick and I know the next words spoken by either of us likely will be volatile, I stick my tongue out at him. And then I wink and say something kind. That's it.

A little humor with a word spoken in love, and World War III is averted.

I guess it's not actually my secret since Solomon wrote something of the same sort thousands of years ago.

Reread Proverbs 15:1 on the previous page, and describe a time in the past when you experienced the truth of each statement.

When a gentle answer turned away wrath:

When a harsh word stirred up anger:

What about lately? When have you been angry, and how have you been hurt? No doubt there is someone who immediately comes to mind. Perhaps this person has betrayed a trust, gossiped about you, or been abusive. We all have hurts. The question is, *When we are hurt, how will we handle it?*

Yesterday's lesson led us to focus on how to respond to criticism in Christlike ways. Today we will expand on those thoughts.

Jesus is our example of how to respond to hurts. Throughout His ministry, He was surrounded by critics and those who plotted to destroy him. The religious leaders attacked Him, and eventually He suffered greatly at their hands. Members of the Sanhedrin conspired against Him, yet He didn't speak up to defend Himself (Mark 14:61). Even His own siblings mocked Him, but He didn't return their insults (John 7:2-9). When faced with opposition, Jesus remained calm and did not retaliate.

Read 1 Peter 2:23 in the margin. What did Jesus do when He was hurt by others?

When he was insulted, he did not answer back with an insult; when he suffered, he did not threaten, but placed his hopes in God, the righteous Judge. (1 Peter 2:23 GNT)

Jesus said, "Father,
forgive them, for
they don't know
what they are
doing." And the
soldiers gambled
for his clothes by
throwing dice.

(Luke 23:34)

────────────

[10]Then the LORD
said to Samuel,
[11]"I am sorry that
I ever made Saul
king, for he has
not been loyal
to me and has
refused to obey my
command."

(1 Samuel
15:10-11a)

────────────

Now the LORD said
to Samuel, "You
have mourned
long enough
for Saul. I have
rejected him as
king of Israel, so
fill your flask with
olive oil and go to
Bethlehem. Find a
man named Jesse
who lives there, for
I have selected one
of his sons to be
my king."

(1 Samuel 16:1)

Also read Luke 23:34 in the margin. What was Jesus' response on the cross to those who were crucifying Him?

In the face of lies, injustice, criticism, persecution, and death, Jesus did not fight back but trusted God to solve the matter. He even asked God to forgive those who were responsible for His death.

This week we are looking at the life of David, who also experienced various hurts. Yesterday we explored some of the ways that he experienced criticism, particularly in his early years. At various times throughout his life, David was attacked and even hunted. One of the most volatile relationships he encountered was with the first king of Israel, Saul. We saw yesterday that God led the prophet Samuel to anoint David as the next king after Saul, but let's fill in the backstory just a bit.

For many years the nation of Israel was led by a series of judges. When the people demanded that God give them a king to rule instead, God directed the prophet Samuel to anoint Saul as their first king. Saul was a great military leader and followed God closely for a time. But as his reign continued, he disobeyed God and did what he chose instead of God's will.

Read 1 Samuel 15:10-11a in the margin. Why was God sorry that He had made Saul king?

Now read 1 Samuel 16:1 in the margin. Why do you think God did not tell Samuel in advance which son of Jesse to anoint? (There is no right or wrong answer here. You might want to look back at yesterday's lesson.)

We know that when the Lord directed Samuel to anoint one of Jesse's sons as the next king, it turned out to be the youngest son, David. And when David bravely faced the giant Goliath—despite opposition from his brother and others—that act of heroism brought him to Saul's attention. For a time David became a constant companion of King Saul and his son, Jonathan. In fact, Jonathan and David developed a deep and lasting friendship.

As David served under Saul's command, God's favor was upon him. This success threatened Saul and made him enraged with jealousy.

Read 1 Samuel 18:28-30 and 19:1a in the margin. What did King Saul's jealousy lead him to do?

Notice that David had done nothing wrong. In fact, he had served Saul faithfully and with great success. But this success, and the love the people of Israel expressed to David, is what fueled Saul's hatred. Saul was plagued with jealousy, insecurity, and personal unfaithfulness—very much as the religious leaders in Jesus' day were. Out of these shortcomings came pain in his own life and the lives of those around him, especially David's.

So, how did David respond as an innocent but wanted man? First, he was shocked. David couldn't believe that the one he had been serving faithfully was really out to hurt him. There was denial, which quickly was replaced with fear when Saul tried to kill David. So he ran. And along the way others joined him—for their own safety and the fact that he was a great leader. For years David lived in hiding. He and his companions often were forced to dwell in caves.

On two occasions while in the wilderness David had the opportunity to kill Saul. His men even encouraged him to do so. Saul's death would have ushered in David's reign as king, ending his nomadic life. Take a moment to look at each situation.

Read 1 Samuel 24:1-7 (page 140) and 1 Samuel 26:7-12. What does David decide to do on each occasion, and what reason does he give?

David had great love and respect for Saul as God's anointed king of Israel and refused to raise a hand against him. Like Jesus in the face of his accusers, David did not choose to retaliate.

18:28When the king realized how much the Lord was with David…, 29he became even more afraid of him and grew to hate him more with every passing day. 30Whenever the Philistine army attacked, David was more successful against them than all the rest of Saul's officers.…

19:1Saul now urged his aides and his son Jonathan to assassinate David.
(1 Samuel 18:28-30; 19:1a TLB)

In the face of lies, injustice, criticism, persecution, and death, Jesus did not fight back but trusted God to solve the matter.

Do you find it hard not to defend yourself when attacked? Why or why not?

Have you ever chosen to remain quiet when falsely accused? If so, what happened?

It's important to recognize that we too have a choice to make when we face difficulties in life. Usually we are unable to control the situations around us, although that's often what we want to do. But what we can do is control our response to those situations.

Here are three biblical principles to help guide us when dealing with hurt:

Listen Carefully

¹⁹You must all be quick to listen, slow to speak, and slow to get angry. ²⁰Human anger does not produce the righteousness God desires. ²¹So get rid of all the filth and evil in your lives, and humbly accept the word God has planted in your hearts, for it has the power to save your souls.

²²But don't just listen to God's word. You must do what it says.

(James 1:19-22)

Forgive Quickly

¹³Bear with each other and forgive one another if any of you has a grievance against someone. Forgive as the Lord forgave you. ¹⁴And over all these virtues put on love, which binds them all together in perfect unity.

(Colossians 3:13-14 NIV)

Love Deeply

Above all, love each other deeply, because love covers over a multitude of sins.

(1 Peter 4:8 NIV)

Rate yourself in each area, putting a check mark in the appropriate column.

	Always	Usually	Sometimes	Nope
1. Listen Carefully				
2. Forgive Quickly				
3. Love Deeply				

Life is not fair. David and Jesus were not treated fairly. David was hunted and Jesus was crucified—not because of any fault of their own. You will not always be treated fairly either. But you always will have the opportunity to choose how to respond when hurts come your way. David chose well in his relationship with Saul. And Jesus chose well at the hands of His persecutors.

So, how will you choose when you face criticism?

What are some practical things you can do in the moment to keep from fighting back or speaking unkindly?

Character wins in the end.

Are there times when God might want us to remain silent when under attack? Explain your response.

Around our house and among the staff of our church, we have a saying that is repeated often: "Character wins in the end." Almost always, when others criticize us unfairly or speak about us unkindly, we can choose not to retaliate. We can choose to speak with kindness or to stay quiet. We can choose not to get into the dirt. In the short term it is often painful, because we would like to set things straight and call people out for their nastiness. But we can know that in the end, character will win.

God is with you when you hurt. When others speak poorly of you or lash out at you, He is close. Allow your heavenly Father to wrap you in His arms in those times and relax in His embrace. From personal experience I can testify that staying quiet in those moments is difficult, but character truly does win in the end!

Pray

- Ask God to help you to listen carefully, forgive quickly, and love deeply those who have hurt you with critical words or actions.
- Thank Jesus for His sacrifice so that you might have forgiveness, and ask God to forgive you for the times when your criticism has hurt others.
- Draw a picture or write your reflections to express what it means to respond like Christ when we are hurt by others.

DAY 3: LEARNING FROM CRITICISM

Settle

Today you might try to find a new space for your time with God. If weather permits, choose a quiet place outside where you can appreciate God's beautiful creation. Or if inside, even a different chair or room can help to create a different experience.

Focus

> Wounds from a friend can be trusted,
> but an enemy multiplies kisses.
> (Proverbs 27:6 NIV)

[5]David was furious. "As surely as the LORD lives," he vowed, "any man who would do such a thing deserves to die! [6]He must repay four lambs to the poor man for the one he stole and for having no pity."

[7]Then Nathan said to David, "You are that man!"
(2 Samuel 12:5-7a)

Reading David's Story (optional): Read 2 Samuel 1–8.

Reflect

One week at church my husband, Jim, and I invited the crowd to ask three close friends this question: *What's it like on the other side of me?* In other words, what's it like to interact and do life with me?

The reaction was overwhelming in several unexpected ways. First, the majority of people said that there is no way they would ever ask anyone that question! It was just too scary. Inviting people to be candid, to reveal blind spots, and to share their insights made them feel too vulnerable. We invited thousands of people to ask the question, but to our knowledge only dozens were willing to give it a try.

The other surprising response was from those who did participate. They too were scared to ask the question, but they moved past the fear and did it anyway; and their learnings were tremendous. Several people, as expected, discovered blind spots and habits that did not bring out their best. One friend shared that she learned new insights from her husband of over forty years. Another friend shared that he had no idea that his witty sarcasm had caused others pain. It was a humbling time for those who had the courage to look for truth.

But the overwhelming surprise for everyone, including me, when we finally got up the courage to ask our friends, spouses, even children, "What's it like on the other side of me?" was that people were mainly positive. The criticism shared was given in love and was constructive. Overall, it was a surprisingly wonderful experience for those who had the courage to do it.

We've established that people are messy. That includes each of us. So being open to constructive criticism in order to become more Christlike is a difficult but helpful trait to have.

One of our focus verses today is Proverbs 27:6. The Amplified Version says it this way: "Faithful are the wounds of a friend [who corrects out of love and concern], / But the kisses of an enemy are deceitful [because they serve his hidden agenda]." In other words, faithful (which means trusted and helpful) are the wounds of criticism we receive from those who love us and have our best interests at heart. Friends of this kind will offer their words of correction in gentleness and will be willing to help us improve. But notice that the word used for their correction is *wounds*. It still hurts, but the difference with wounds from a friend is that they do not leave us hopeless and alone. A friend walks with us through the process of repentance and encourages us to live in new and better ways. Wounds from an enemy, on the other hand, just leave us hurting and vulnerable.

We need people in our lives who can speak deep truths to us—even when those truths are constructive criticism.

When and how have wounds from a friend been helpful in your life?

Whom do you trust to answer the question *What's it like on the other side of me?*

In David's life, most of the criticism he received stemmed from the jealousy of others, but in 2 Samuel 12 we read of a time when he received constructive criticism from the prophet Nathan. Before we get to that, though, we need to know the backstory.

In 2 Samuel 11, we learn that David lusted after another man's wife. Her name was Bathsheba, and her husband was Uriah. While Uriah was away in battle, David had Bathsheba brought to his palace and slept with her; and she became pregnant. David went to great lengths to hide his sins; but when that failed, he devised a plan to have Uriah killed in combat. He then brought Bathsheba into his home as his wife, hoping that no one would learn of his transgressions. The last verse of chapter 11 tells us that "the LORD was displeased with what David had done" (v. 27). In the next chapter, we read:

> ¹So the LORD sent Nathan the prophet to tell David this story: "There were two men in a certain town. One was rich, and one was poor. ²The rich man owned a great many sheep and cattle. ³The poor man owned nothing but one little lamb he had bought. He raised that little lamb, and it grew up with his children. It ate from the man's own plate and drank from his cup. He cuddled it in his arms like a baby daughter. ⁴One day a guest arrived at the home of the rich man. But instead of killing an animal from his own flock or herd, he took the poor man's lamb and killed it and prepared it for his guest."

> ⁵David was furious. "As surely as the LORD lives," he vowed, "any man who would do such a thing deserves to die! ⁶He must repay four lambs to the poor man for the one he stole and for having no pity."

> ⁷Then Nathan said to David, "You are that man! The LORD, the God of Israel, says: I anointed you king of Israel and saved you from the power of Saul. ⁸I gave you your master's house and his wives and the kingdoms of Israel and Judah. And if that had not been enough, I would have given you much, much more. ⁹Why, then, have you despised the word of the LORD and done this horrible deed? For you have murdered Uriah the Hittite with the sword of the Ammonites and stolen his wife. ¹⁰From this time on, your family will live by the sword because you have despised me by taking Uriah's wife to be your own.

> ¹¹"This is what the LORD says: Because of what you have done, I will cause your own household to rebel against you. I will give your wives to another man before your very eyes, and he will go to bed with them in public view. ¹²You did it secretly, but I will make this happen to you openly in the sight of all Israel."

Motive, timing, attitude, and wording are critical in doing the right thing in the right way.

¹³Then David confessed to Nathan, "I have sinned against the LORD."

Nathan replied, "Yes, but the LORD has forgiven you, and you won't die for this sin."

(2 Samuel 12:1-13)

What stands out to you in this encounter? What can we learn for our own experiences with constructive criticism—whether we're on the giving or receiving end?

There is much to be learned from this encounter. Some of the most important words we read here are the first ones: "So the LORD sent Nathan" (v. 1). Nathan did not go in his own timing or with his own motive. He waited until he was sent by the Lord. Motive, timing, attitude, and wording are critical in doing the right thing in the right way. Nathan went because the Lord asked him to go—and when the Lord sent him. Not before. He approached David in a wise and gentle way, first by telling a story and then by confronting David with his sin. He also offered hope and forgiveness from the Lord at the end of the encounter. What a great example to us of how to be used by God. Nathan stayed close to the Lord throughout this whole situation. This, friend, is a great example for us to use when we feel led to confront someone with an issue in their life.

Do you generally wait for the Lord to tell you if, when, and how to give critical feedback, or do you tend to forge ahead on your own? Why is it important to wait on the Lord?

How would you describe the tone you tend to use when you offer criticism?

Read Proverbs 9:8-9 in the margin. According to these verses, what kind of person receives correction and what kind does not? When we respond to correction by receiving it, what is the outcome?

[8] *So don't bother correcting mockers; they will only hate you. But correct the wise, and they will love you.* [9] *Instruct the wise, and they will be even wiser. Teach the righteous, and they will learn even more.*
(Proverbs 9:8-9)

Let's consider David's and Nathan's responses to the confrontation. David did not make excuses or become angry when his sins were revealed. He was repentant. He accepted the consequences for his disobedience, which were severe. But he also welcomed the forgiveness of the God he loved.

Then there is Nathan's response. He obediently delivered a difficult message to someone in authority. In verse 11 we read, "This is what the LORD says." Nathan delivered God's message, not his own. He stuck with the script given to him by the Lord without offering his own opinions and commentary.

Even when you feel led by God to confront someone, be careful to say only what God is leading you to say. Don't ad-lib. A life verse for me, among many, is Proverbs 10:19 (HCSB): "When there are many words, sin is unavoidable." This is such a practical and powerful verse. Learning when and how to speak is a mark of maturity in faith.

The other response we see from Nathan is that he did not abandon his friend David after revealing these grievous sins. He walked with him through the consequences and the redemption. Proverbs 18:24 (NKJV) says, "There is a friend who sticks closer than a brother." King Solomon, one of David's sons, wrote that. Perhaps it was his father's friendship with Nathan that inspired this Proverb.

David and Nathan loved the Lord and each other deeply, and that love allowed them to weather difficult conversations. In fact, 1 Chronicles 3:5 tells us that King David and Bathsheba later named one of their sons Nathan. No doubt the child's name was a reflection of their appreciation for Nathan's faithfulness, friendship, and courageous love through the years.

Are you willing to walk with your friends through the process when you offer criticism? Explain your response.

Learning when and how to speak is a mark of maturity in faith.

An unreliable
messenger stumbles
into trouble,
  but a reliable
  messenger
  brings healing.
    (Proverbs 13:17)

As iron sharpens iron,
  so a friend
  sharpens a friend.
    (Proverbs 27:17)

Read Proverbs 13:17 and Proverbs 27:17 in the margin. What do these Scriptures teach us about the types of people we should choose for close friendships?

A mature believer is one who surrounds herself with a few trusted friends who have permission to speak truths, even the hard ones, into her life. Take the time to develop those relationships that can allow you to grow and learn through godly critique.

Pray

- Greet the Lord with thanksgiving for who He is today. Perhaps you could sing a song of praise to God as part of your prayer to Him.
- Thank Him for the trusted friends in your life. Take time to list the names of these friends and ask for God's blessings in their lives. If you need friends like this in your life, ask God for them.
- Ask God to help you be open to constructive feedback from others and to follow His lead and timing for sharing that kind of feedback with others.

DAY 4: EVALUATING THE CRITIQUE

Settle

Begin your time with God by listening to "Waiting Here for You," recorded by Christy Nockels, or another song of praise of your choice.

Focus

A *perverse person stirs up conflict,*
> *And a gossip separates close friends.*
>> *(Proverbs 16:28 NIV)*

But while he [Absalom] was there, he sent secret messengers to all the tribes of Israel to stir up a rebellion against the king. "As soon as you hear the ram's horn," his message read, "you are to say, 'Absalom has been crowned king in Hebron.' "

(2 Samuel 15:10)

Reading David's Story (optional): Read 2 Samuel 9–16.

Reflect

When our family moved to a new area to start a nontraditional church, there was a lot of criticism from other Christians in the community. Casual dress, drums, and meeting in rented spaces seemed to be the most popular topics of criticism. But at a more personal level, there were times when the comments were unkind and aimed at my family. Ouch!

For instance, in the absence of a church office during those early years, I would spend my Thursday mornings at the local office supply store printing programs for the weekend. Usually I had at least one toddler in tow, and the staff of the store would play with the kids. Eventually we all became friends. One day while printing, a couple walked up and said, "We noticed that you are working on the bulletin for that new church." So I got excited and asked, "Do you have a church home?" I thought I might get to invite them to our church. But the conversation took a different turn, because next they said, "Oh, yes. We have a church, but we've heard about that couple starting that new church." I thought, *That couple...you mean me and my sweet husband.* I responded with interest, "Really? Tell me about them." At this point the printing clerk perked up and stepped over to see how this conversation was going to go. The couple went on to say things like, "Well, you know they're meeting in a hotel, not a real church. It seems kind of cultic if you ask us. He doesn't even wear a robe. There are drums! Also, we've heard they will let just anybody in to worship." And so it went on and on.

Finally I said, "Well, from what I know, they love the Lord and are intent on reaching people far from God with the love of Jesus." It was a painful yet awkwardly funny conversation. As I left, I scooped up my kids and the programs, turned to the clerk, and said, "After I leave, feel free to tell them who we are."

In those first days of starting the church, the criticism was really hard for me. It hurt my feelings and left me discouraged. In fact, there were times when I was tempted to give up on the vision of starting this new church. There was a season when I wanted to walk away from God's invitation to do ministry with Him because of the pain of criticism.

It was during that time that my husband, Jim, gave me some great advice: "Don't worry about the Christian critics; they're not our target. Our target audience is those who are far from God. Just keep doing what God told us to do." In other words, don't let anything distract you from God's mission!

We all have things that distract us from God's calling in our lives.

Read Matthew 14:22-32. What is Peter's "calling" in this story?

When the disciple Peter stepped out of the boat, he was able to walk on water because he was focused on responding to his Master's voice. But when his focus shifted from Jesus to the wind and the waves, he began to sink. There's a great lesson here for us!

What distracts you from focusing on God?

How can you focus your life and time this week on what God has called you to do?

David had to learn when to ignore criticism, such as when his own brothers mocked his bravery in confronting Goliath, and when to listen, such as he did when the prophet Nathan confronted him with his sins of adultery and murder. And we must learn to do the same. The key is in evaluating the source or motivation of the critic.

Earlier this week we explored the story of David and Goliath in 1 Samuel 17, but let's revisit it now through the lens of evaluating the critic. As we saw, David was sent to the battlefield to check on his brothers, who were preparing to fight the Philistines. When he arrived he found a standoff between Goliath, a champion fighter of the enemy, and the Israelite army. Goliath had issued a challenge to one-on-one combat, but no one in the Israelite camp was willing to take on the giant—that is, until young David arrived.

David was shocked at the fear he saw among the Israelites. He was embarrassed that no one had come forward. So he volunteered himself. As a shepherd, God had helped David defeat both the bear and the lion, so he figured that surely God would be with him to fight just one man. But those closest to him mocked his courage and intentions.

> **Read 1 Samuel 17:28 in the margin. Based on what you read here, what would you say is Eliab's motivation for the criticism he directed at David?**

When Eliab, David's oldest brother, heard him speaking with the men, he burned with anger at him and asked, "Why have you come down here? And with whom did you leave those few sheep in the wilderness? I know how conceited you are and how wicked your heart is; you came down only to watch the battle."
(1 Samuel 17:28 NIV)

Not only did Eliab accuse David of just wanting to see the blood and gore, he also questioned David's motives. But David didn't focus on his brother. His focus was on the strength of God. He just ignored his brother and the other naysayers and took on Goliath. David listened to his brother, evaluated his intentions, and then chose to focus on the giant instead of the critics. What David did—and what Jim taught me in the face of my critics—was to evaluate the source and not become distracted.

David's son Absalom was another great critic. His goal was to overthrow his father's rule and take the throne for himself. In 2 Samuel 15–18 we see that he plotted to destroy David. We also see the turmoil that David endured as a father who tried to restore a relationship with his son but had to come to terms with his son's wicked intentions. In the case with Absalom we see

"Then we must flee at once, or it will be too late!" David urged his men. "Hurry! If we get out of the city before Absalom arrives, both we and the city of Jerusalem will be spared from disaster."

(2 Samuel 15:14)

If people are causing divisions among you, give a first and second warning. After that, have nothing more to do with them.

(Titus 3:10)

a critic with jealous and evil motives. But David's love for his son seemingly blinded him from seeing the situation clearly. His parental love clouded good judgment and ultimately led to a disastrous outcome.

Read 2 Samuel 15:14 in the margin. What was the crisis point that resulted from David's blindness toward the situation with Absalom? How might this story have ended differently if David had confronted Absalom earlier in life?

In more general terms, how might love for a child cloud a parent's judgment?

Now read Titus 3:10 in the margin. How can this Scripture guide you in dealing with your critics?

David's brother and his son Absalom criticized him with a motive of jealousy, just as King Saul did as we saw on Day 2. Although these were painful situations, David had to evaluate the source or motivation of their critiques in order to move forward in wisdom.

All criticism is not created equally. Some is meant to sharpen us; some is meant to hurt us. Some comes from jealousy and attempts to distract us from completing what God has called us to do; some comes from a deeply rooted love. There is wisdom in evaluating the criticism we receive in order to determine the motivation so that we can know what to keep and what to discard.

Before jumping to conclusions, we must be sure we've taken the time to listen carefully, and then we can consider if the critique is actually a blind spot in our life. Seeking counsel from trusted friends will help us identify

if the critique is a truth meant to help us or something more devious in nature.

Recall a time recently when you were criticized or critiqued. Do you believe it was meant to help or to hurt, and why? What do you think was the person's motivation?

List one or more trusted friends you can to turn to for help when evaluating criticism:

Here are a few Scriptures and questions that can guide us when it comes to evaluating the critique of our critics:

Scriptures

Fools think their own way is right,
*   but the wise listen to others.*
*   (Proverbs 12:15)*

If you stop listening to instruction, my child,
*   you will turn your back on knowledge.*
*   (Proverbs 19:27)*

"If your brother or sister sins, go and point out their fault, just between the two of you. If they listen to you, you have won them over.
*   (Matthew 18:15 NIV)*

⁴Love is patient, love is kind. It does not envy, it does not boast, it is not proud. ⁵It does not dishonor others, it is not self-seeking, it is not

> **All criticism is not created equally. Some is meant to sharpen us; some is meant to hurt us.**

easily angered, it keeps no record of wrongs. ⁶Love does not delight in evil but rejoices with the truth. ⁷It always protects, always trusts, always hopes, always perseveres.

(1 Corinthians 13:4-7 NIV)

Questions

Was the criticism offered in love and kindness as described in 1 Corinthians 13?

Was it offered privately, rather than publicly?

Did the person come to you directly, rather than speaking through others?

Is the person willing to walk through the correction with you?

Was the critique offered in an attempt to help you, rather than hurt you?

If the answer to one or more of these questions is no, then run! Or at the very least, evaluate what may be going on here. Is there jealousy or another not-so-admirable motivation? In order to become the best version of yourself, you need trusted people who can speak honestly into your life. However, you also need wisdom to know whether a critic is one of those people and what his or her motivation is.

Wisdom is looking at life from God's perspective. As you face criticism, and as you offer it, let wisdom and God's love be your guides.

Pray

- Thank God for His constant presence in your life.
- In James 1:5 we are told that if we ask for wisdom, God will gladly give it. Ask Him for wisdom as you discern the critics facing you.
- Surrender any grudges you may be holding toward those who have been critical of you in the past.

DAY 5: MOVING PAST YOUR CRITICS

Settle

What calms your spirit? Try something new today that brings you joy—coloring, sketching, playing an instrument, singing, exercising. Do that today "as to the Lord" (Colossians 3:23 KJV).

Focus

The tongue of the wise adorns knowledge,
*   but the mouth of the fool gushes folly.*
*   (Proverbs 15:2 NIV)*

[14]And David danced before the LORD with all his might, wearing a priestly garment. [15]So David and all the people of Israel brought up the Ark of the LORD with shouts of joy and the blowing of rams' horns.

[16]But as the Ark of the LORD entered the City of David, Michal, the daughter of Saul, looked down from her window. When she saw King David leaping and dancing before the LORD, she was filled with contempt for him.

[20] . . . Michal, the daughter of Saul, came out to meet him. She said in disgust, "How distinguished the king of Israel looked today, shamelessly exposing himself to the servant girls like any vulgar person might do!"

[21]David retorted . . . [22]"I am willing to look even more foolish than this, even to be humiliated in my own eyes!"

(2 Samuel 6:14-16, 20-22)

Reading David's Story (optional): Read 2 Samuel 17–24.

Reflect

As I shared yesterday, the first days of church planting brought a lot of criticism. One day as I was laying my son down for a nap, there was a knock on the door. It was a pastor from the area, someone we had known from afar for years. He had stopped by to say that he had heard about the work we were doing and the more contemporary style of service we were offering to the community. He went on to say, "A church that doesn't sing 'When I Survey the Wondrous Cross' is actually not a church at all." I tried to explain our goals and what we were trying to accomplish by reaching people far from God. He wasn't interested.

After he left, I just sat at the kitchen table on the edge of tears, waiting for Jim to come home. Surely he would be discouraged. What would this mean for us?

When Jim walked in the door an hour later, I sat him down and shared about our visitor. He got up, poured himself some juice, and said, "That's okay. He's already going to heaven. Don't worry about it. God didn't tell us to build a church for guys like him."

That was the whole discussion. Jim didn't call the pastor to defend himself. He didn't have a mini-breakdown. In fact, the only time he spent defending himself was to me by saying, "Don't worry about it." He just poured juice and moved on.

Jim has always had a steadfastness about what God has called him to do. He just doesn't waver. He calls it answering to his audience of One. I try to live the same way, but if I'm honest, at times I take my eyes off of the One and become concerned with the detractors. That concern often serves to prevent me from serving God at my best.

In 2 Samuel 6 we read the account of David dancing and praising the Lord as the ark of the covenant is brought into Jerusalem. As his wife Michal looks down from her window and sees David rejoicing, she is not pleased with what she views as un-kingly behavior. She is critical, even showing disgust and contempt for David. But he is not swayed.

Reread 2 Samuel 6:22 (page 160). What was David's response to Michal's criticism? What do you think he meant by this?

I like how *The Message* puts it: "Oh yes, I'll dance to God's glory—more recklessly even than this. And as far as I'm concerned . . . I'll gladly look like a fool."

*The tongue of
the wise adorns
knowledge,
but the mouth
of the fool
gushes folly.
(Proverbs 15:2 NIV)*

Have you ever looked like a fool for God? If so, when and how?

**Read Proverbs 15:2 in the margin. According to this verse, who
was the real fool—Michal or David? Explain your answer.**

**If we keep
our eyes on
God we can
overcome
criticism with
confidence.**

Michal gushed foolishness and negativity. But David chose to celebrate
God's favor. Rather than focusing on the voice of criticism, even from his
own spouse, he chose to focus on pleasing God.

Like Michal, negative people can be distractions. If we're not careful,
they can take our focus off of God's plan and leave us consumed with
defending ourselves or wallowing in self-doubt. When God gives us an
important assignment, there are sure to be naysayers telling us that we're
the wrong person, we've got the wrong idea, we're doing it the wrong way, or
we're just not good enough. But like David, if we keep our eyes on God we
can overcome criticism with confidence.

David is not the only biblical character to endure harsh criticism and
move past his critics. Moses, Mordecai, Joseph, Job, and Nehemiah are
other examples of those who overcame the negativity of others in order to
achieve God's will. They moved past their critics in order to focus on God's
objectives.

Take Nehemiah, for example. Nehemiah wasn't a preacher or a builder.
He was a Jewish refugee who had risen to a level of prestige as a cup bearer
to the king of a foreign land. Decades ago Israel had been taken captive
by the Babylonians, and in the process Jerusalem had been destroyed. The
strongest and brightest of Israel had been deported to Babylon. Those who
were left in Israel were defenseless and in need. The Israelites were held in
exile for seventy years, and then they were allowed to journey back home.

When word from the first travelers reached Nehemiah, announcing
that his homeland had been destroyed and that those living there were
defenseless, it broke his heart. He cried out to God on their behalf and was
given the huge task to go home and rebuild the city wall in order to protect

those living in Jerusalem. It was a massive undertaking, but Nehemiah knew it was God leading him to do it.

When Nehemiah asked the Persian king for permission to return to help his people, he was given the time and even the resources to accomplish the task. But there were those closer to home who were not as supportive. They had benefited from Jerusalem being left desolate, and Nehemiah's plans to rebuild were not in their best interests. So they began to criticize. Nehemiah's enemies resorted to ridicule, insults, rumors, and even threats of violence to stop him from rebuilding the wall around Jerusalem. When none of that worked, they tried to slow him down with discussion.

Nehemiah, however, knew clearly what God had called him to do, and he would not be distracted.

Read Nehemiah 6:1-4. What did Nehemiah's enemies want him to do, and what was his reply?

When they sent the same message four times, what did Nehemiah do?

When Nehemiah's detractors wanted to slow the progress of the construction, they sent him messages asking him to meet with them—four different times! Each time he gave the same reply, telling them he was doing a great work and could not stop to meet with them.

I wish Nehemiah's response here had come to mind the day I sat at my kitchen table in tears. It would have spared me some turmoil if I, like Nehemiah and King David, had been more focused on God's voice than on the detractors around me.

Every great opportunity comes with opposition. When we attempt anything of significance in life, there will be someone who opposes our progress. We must learn the delicate balance of being open to correction from trusted sources while remaining steadfast in moving forward with God's mission in spite of opposition.

When offered and received in love, criticism can be an integral tool in how we grow.

When have you felt God directing you to a new opportunity?

What opposition did you encounter, and how did you handle it?

What would you do differently if you had it to do over?

Years ago I read a short article titled "Don't Spend Your Life with Your Critics," by Tim Stevens and Tony Morgan.[2] It was a simple but eye-opening read for me. Let me share a little of it with you in hopes that it may help you also:

> I used to think that I needed to take the time to convince every critical person to see things my way. I was also convinced that if I just talked to these folks long enough, I could change their thinking....I soon learned I was wrong. I was just wasting precious minutes God had given me to invest in meaningful and effective ministry. Answering every criticism and explaining every questioned action will wear you out!...You need to filter your critics.

Amen to that! This little article changed the way I did ministry and life. Is it important to be open to feedback? Absolutely! When offered and received in love, criticism can be an integral tool in how we grow. However, spending too much time responding to every critic will leave you weary and rarely will move you forward to accomplish what God has called you to do.

Your critics will use the same tactics employed against Nehemiah to prevent you from achieving what God has for your life. They'll ridicule you, spread rumors about you, doubt you, and even threaten you to get you to stop doing what God wants you to do. Do it anyway! Be brave!

Nehemiah and David did not allow their detractors to keep them from accomplishing what God had called them to do. There will be those who are threatened by you. Others will be jealous of your success. When gossip, ridicule, or even lies come at you, don't despair. Let God handle it. Remember, character wins in the end. Like these great biblical heroes, allow God to be your advocate, protector, Savior, defender, and champion.

Pray

- Commit yourself to living for an audience of One, God.
- Take time to pray for and forgive those who have hurt you through criticism in the past.
- Seek God's courage to move past the things that discourage you and hold you back in order to live boldly and joyfully for Christ.
- Perhaps, like David, you might even dance before the Lord as part of your prayer time. Do it! Have fun!

Death and life are in the power of the tongue.

(Proverbs 18:21a NKJV)

Whoever restrains his words has knowledge,

and he who has a cool spirit is a man of understanding.

(Proverbs 17:27 ESV)

1. Listen _____.

If you reject discipline, you only harm yourself;

but if you listen to correction, you grow in understanding.

(Proverbs 15:32)

Wounds from a friend can be trusted,

but an enemy multiplies kisses.

(Proverbs 27:6 NIV)

2. Stay _____.

Fools give full vent to their rage,

but the wise bring calm in the end.

(Proverbs 29:11 NIV)

VIDEO VIEWER GUIDE: WEEK 5

A soft answer turns away wrath,
But a harsh word stirs up anger.
> (Proverbs 15:1 NKJV)

When words are many, transgression is not lacking.
> (Proverbs 10:19a ESV)

3. Process the _____.

In the multitude of counselors there is victory.
(Proverbs 11:14b New Heart English Bible)

4. Learn _____ _____ _____.

5. _____ about it.

Do not nag your children. If you are too hard to please, they may want to stop trying.
> (Colossians 3:21 NCV)

Therefore encourage one another and build each other up, just as in fact you are doing.
> (1 Thessalonians 5:11 NIV)

Week 6

Daniel

Thriving in Messy Circumstances

Daniel 1–3

DAY 1: RESOLVING TO BE DISCIPLINED

Settle

Where do you experience God's presence most powerfully? Maybe it's by the ocean, in the mountains, or in your own backyard. Picture yourself in that spot, and allow the peace and presence of God in that setting to invade your soul.

Focus

No discipline seems pleasant at the time, but painful. Later on, however, it produces a harvest of righteousness and peace for those who have been trained by it.

(Hebrews 12:11 NIV)

⁵The king assigned them a daily ration of the best food and wine from his own kitchens. They were to be trained for three years, and then they would enter the royal service. . . . ⁸But Daniel was determined not to defile himself by eating the food and wine given to them by the king. He asked the chief of staff for permission not to eat these unacceptable foods.

(Daniel 1:5, 8)

Reading Daniel's Story (optional): The Book of Daniel has twelve chapters. If you haven't read it recently—or perhaps ever—you may want to take time to read it this week. Just three chapters a day and you'll have it done by the fourth day! Today, read Daniel 1–3.

Reflect

There are two verses that come to mind often as I'm going about my daily activities. The first is one of our focus verses for today, and the other is a proverb:

No discipline seems pleasant at the time, but painful. Later on, however, it produces a harvest of righteousness and peace for those who have been trained by it.

(Hebrews 12:11 NIV)

Sin is not ended by multiplying words,
but the prudent hold their tongues.
(*Proverbs* 10:19 NIV)

When I'm ordering in the drive-thru line, hearing gossip, or trying to decide whether to go to the gym, these verses pop into my mind, reminding me to practice discipline! Whether I'm dealing with my attitude, eating and spending habits, or frustrations, there they are again! These words from Scripture help me to be disciplined in my responses (most of the time). In fact, these two passages have helped me to discipline my tongue and my actions for many years.

How could living by these two verses bring discipline and blessing into your life?

In what ways might you need to endure pain for a time in order to discipline yourself in ways that bring honor to God?

This week we will be considering the messy life circumstances of Daniel—a young man who loved the Lord and sought to honor Him in difficult situations. Daniel was born at a time in history when Israel was entrenched in idolatry. Pagan idol worship, sexual immorality, and injustice had become a way of life among God's people. Prophets of the Lord such as Jeremiah, Isaiah, and Zephaniah had warned the Israelites to turn away from these sins, but the people had not listened. As a nation they remained unfaithful to God.

So God allowed the Israelites to be conquered in order to get their attention and turn their hearts back to Him. About 2,600 years ago, in 586 BC, Jerusalem fell to the Babylonians.[1] Daniel was a young man when the army of King Nebuchadnezzar, the most powerful man in the world at the time, conquered the Israelites' capital city. After Jerusalem was destroyed, Nebuchadnezzar took back with him to Babylon (which is modern-day Iraq) some of Israel's finest young men.

Read Daniel 1:4 in the margin. What were the king's criteria for the selection of these young men?

What kind of training were they to receive?

"Select only strong, healthy, and good-looking young men," he said. "Make sure they are well versed in every branch of learning, are gifted with knowledge and good judgment, and are suited to serve in the royal palace. Train these young men in the language and literature of Babylon."

(Daniel 1:4)

King Nebuchadnezzar wanted the brightest, best-looking, and most educated young men of Israel. Daniel was one of these prisoners of war. Separated from his parents and taken from his home, he was trained in Babylonian culture, including the language, politics, and pagan practices. Babylon was even more wicked than his homeland of Israel. Daniel's life, through no fault of his own, became very messy. But with God's help, he found a way to honor the God of Israel and thrive in his difficult situation.

Our lives are going to have messy, painful times as well. Sometimes they are the direct result of our own poor choices—a poorly chosen word, a bad decision, or an unhealthy lifestyle. But other times life becomes painful through no fault of our own. Either way the question is, Will we thrive in our messy circumstances as Daniel did?

This week as we explore the life of Daniel (including his three friends Shadrach, Meshach, and Abednego), we will dig into five character values that can help us navigate messy circumstances:

1. Discipline
2. Humility
3. Integrity
4. Wisdom
5. Courage

Today we are concentrating on the first characteristic, discipline, as we look at the first major problem Daniel encountered shortly after arriving in Babylon.

As prisoners of war, Daniel and the other young men were placed in a three-year Babylonian indoctrination program. They were given new names, a new language, and even a new diet.

Reread Daniel 1:5, 8 (page 169). What were they given to eat and drink, and what was Daniel's response?

As he sought to thrive in Babylon, Daniel's first dilemma was how to handle his diet. No more kosher food, prepared according to the Levitical dietary standards. Eating the food from the king's table was a line Daniel felt he could not cross, and he "was determined not to defile himself" (v. 8). Some translations say that he resolved or purposed in his heart not to defile himself (NIV, NKJV). I love that. Daniel chose. He was intentional and made the decision not to conform when it came to choices that he believed would not honor God. That, in and of itself, required discipline.

Surely as a young man living away from family for the first time, the rich foods and wine of the king's table were tempting. He and his companions were free to consume as much as they chose. Like a young person going off to college for the first time, Daniel and his posse could have indulged in all kinds of wickedness and partying. But Daniel had resolve.

Here's how Daniel handled the dilemma. He talked it over with the chief official or palace master that he and his three friends reported to, offering a suggestion:

> 12"Please test us for ten days on a diet of vegetables and water," Daniel said. 13"At the end of the ten days, see how we look compared to the other young men who are eating the king's food. Then make your decision in light of what you see." 14The attendant agreed....

> 15At the end of the ten days, Daniel and his three friends looked healthier and better nourished than the young men who had been eating the food assigned by the king....

> 18When the training period ordered by the king was completed,... 19...no one impressed him as much as Daniel, Hananiah, Mishael, and Azariah. So they entered the royal service.

> (Daniel 1:12-19)

How did Daniel's experiment require discipline?

How did God reward him for this discipline?

"You must not follow the crowd in doing wrong.... Do not be swayed by the crowd."
(Exodus 23:2)

When faced with something that would force him to compromise his values in order to conform, Daniel resolved not to do it. He was not abrasive in how he handled the situation but humbly found a way to be true to God without offending those in authority. He was a young man of deep integrity and humility who displayed wisdom far beyond his years. And as a result of Daniel's discipline, he and his faithful friends were rewarded in the end.

Read Exodus 23:2 and Romans 12:2 in the margin and answer the following questions:

What do these verses urge us not to do?

Don't copy the behavior and customs of this world, but let God transform you into a new person by changing the way you think. Then you will learn to know God's will for you, which is good and pleasing and perfect.
(Romans 12:2)

When and how have you been swayed by the crowd in the past?

When have you taken a stand against culture, and how has it affected your life?

As Christians living in our culture today, how can we relate to Daniel's situation in Babylon?

What are some challenges we face as individuals and as the church in not conforming to the values of this world?

Instead of blending in with the culture, we must resolve . . . to honor God in every area of our lives if we want to thrive.

Daniel is a good example of how to live in a disciplined, winsome way in a hostile, messy world. His reality, like ours today, was an environment that did not honor godly values. As Daniel handled this first challenge, he demonstrated not only discipline but also humility, integrity, wisdom, and courage—characteristics that he would employ in future difficulties as well. We will continue digging into these characteristics as we explore more of Daniel's life throughout the week.

As Christ-followers, we too are often tempted to give in to things around us. But instead of blending in with the culture, we must resolve as Daniel did to honor God in every area of our lives if we want to thrive.

Pray

- Consider what areas of your life need discipline. How can you commit these areas to the Lord today as a matter of prayer and practical application?
- Thank God for the gift of His Word that teaches, guides, encourages, and corrects us.
- Just be still before God and allow Him to speak to your heart today.

DAY 2: DISPLAYING TRUE HUMILITY

Settle

Close your eyes and let your head fall gently to the right while pressing down on your left temple with your right hand; then do the same thing on the other side, pressing down on your right temple with your left hand. This is a great stress reliever as you slow down to focus your whole attention on the Lord.

Focus

Finally, everyone must live in harmony, be sympathetic, love each other, have compassion, and be humble.

(1 Peter 3:8 GW)

[16]Daniel went at once to see the king and requested more time to tell the king what the dream meant.

[17]Then Daniel went home and told his friends Hananiah, Mishael, and Azariah what had happened. [18]He urged them to ask the God of heaven to show them his mercy by telling them the secret, so they would not be executed along with the other wise men of Babylon. [19]That night the secret was revealed to Daniel in a vision. Then Daniel praised the God of heaven.

(Daniel 2:16-19)

Reading Daniel's Story (optional): Read Daniel 4–6.

Reflect

While getting my hair cut recently, my new stylist said, "I'm so glad to get to know you. I always thought you were distant and hard to approach. But just in these few minutes, I see you in a whole new light. You should be more outgoing so people can really see who you are." She was smiling and even gave me a little hug as she said this, but I was devastated. Literally, my eyes filled with tears, and I pretended to have a sudden need to go to the bathroom in order to get myself together. Distant, hard to approach—these were like steel daggers to my heart. This is the opposite of who I want to be!

After thinking—way too much—about this encounter, I realized that there are times when I put up a wall in public and just get quiet. Apparently, that quietness may be perceived as snobby or even mean, which was news to me. My husband, Jim, by comparison, is the life of the party. He never meets a stranger. Truly, he has wet puppy syndrome: he's excited about each new person who walks in the door.

Through reflecting on my hairstylist's comments, I learned that over my years in ministry—which have included many bumps, bruises, and hurts along the way—I had put up a wall. I didn't want to let people in too close until I knew it was safe. This wasn't my true nature but a learned skill or defense mechanism to protect myself and my kids.

This hairstylist gave me a new view into the mirror of my life. As a result, I've become more affectionate and outgoing. Now I take the initiative, most of the time, to be friendly first. It's hard. It stretches me. But I have realized that if I want to represent Christ well, these are some habits I need to weave into my life.

Seeing ourselves clearly is hard. No matter how keen our eyesight is, it can be difficult to see ourselves in our own mirrors, so to speak. I'm not talking about being able to see the physical reality of ourselves in a mirror, although sometimes that can be fuzzy to us also. I'm talking about seeing our own character strengths and weaknesses when we examine our "reflection"— the way others see us. For example, when gazing into the mirror, few people see themselves as selfish or arrogant. And those who are truly humble, kind, and unselfish probably would not claim those characteristics either.

What has been revealed in the past about your nature or character that was a surprise to you?

This week we are looking at five characteristics that Daniel (and his friends) demonstrated in the midst of his messy circumstances, and today we are focusing on humility. Humility is one of those things that is hard to recognize "in the mirror." I mean, if you recognize your humility and are proud of it, then maybe you don't actually have it, right? Can we be proud of our humility? Probably not, because the opposite of humility is pride.

Pride is very hard to see in ourselves. Though others can easily see it, the mirror rarely reflects it accurately for us. In fact, pride often can be deceptive, showing up as stubbornness, arrogance, criticism, or competition. And it can be dangerous.

Pride leads to destruction;
a proud attitude brings ruin.
(Proverbs 16:18 NCV)

Read Proverbs 16:18 in the margin. What does pride destroy?

We might say that pride is a deadly sickness and humility is its antidote. Pride destroys relationships, but humility builds them up. Humility allows conversation and leads to connection and loving compassion.

Reread 1 Peter 3:8 (page 175). What character qualities does this verse encourage?

Godly friends can help shape us into the persons God wants us to be.

Why is humility necessary if we are to live in harmony— demonstrating sympathy, love, and compassion?

Do you have the courage to ask a few trusted friends if this verse describes you? If so, record their responses below:

Because it is difficult to see ourselves clearly, asking a trusted friend to give some honest insights can be helpful. Then we can begin to work on those areas where we may be lacking, including humility.

Godly friends can help shape us into the persons God wants us to be. I recently saw a social media post that said, "Real queens quietly straighten one another's crowns." That's awesome. I need some people to quietly come alongside me when my tiara gets tilted and help me get back on track. Having people in our lives who love us enough to speak truthfully is a blessing.

On the other hand, if we aren't intentional about hanging out with people who love God and want to see us live our very best lives, we can fall into trouble. As 1 Corinthians 15:33 (NIV) reminds us, "Do not be misled: 'Bad company corrupts good character.' " This is a practical warning from Scripture. Even when our intentions are honorable, our character can be damaged by hanging out with people with poor morals.

A key to shaping our character, then, is paying attention to who we hang out with. If we want to incorporate the five characteristics of Daniel into our lives—discipline, humility, integrity, wisdom, and courage—we need to hang out with those who display these traits.

Take a good look at your three closest friends. What are five predominant traits you see among them?

1.

2.

3.

4.

5.

Did humility make the list? If not, what insight or understanding might this reveal?

Which of these traits describe yourself as well?

Are these traits a good representation of Christ's likeness? Why or why not?

Based on this exercise, what character trait might you want to work on this week? What can you do, with the help of the Holy Spirit, to grow in this area?

We saw in chapter 1 that Daniel distinguished himself through discipline and found favor in the king's eyes, being appointed as a trusted advisor. In chapter 2, we see that by necessity Daniel finds himself facing a unique challenge: interpreting King Nebuchadnezzar's dream.

Read Daniel 2:1-15 and answer the following questions:

What did the king ask of his advisors—his magicians, enchanters, sorcerers, and astrologers?

What would be the consequence if they could not fulfill his request?

How did they respond initially, and what did they say when the king insisted?

What was the king's response, and how did Daniel handle the situation?

The king wanted his advisors to interpret his dream, but he would not share the dream with them because he wanted them to prove their powers by divining from their sources not only the interpretation of the dream but also the dream itself. When they could not meet this impossible challenge, the king ordered that all of his advisors, including Daniel and his friends, be killed. But Daniel took action.

Reread Daniel 2:16-19 (page 175). How do we see both humility and courage in Daniel's actions? What was the outcome?

Daniel went before the king and humbly pleaded with him for more time to seek answers to the dream and its meaning. He then asked his three God-fearing friends to join him in humbly asking the Lord for help. During the night God revealed and explained the mystery of the dream to Daniel in a vision, and he praised the God of heaven.

Read Daniel 2:20-23. What stands out to you in Daniel's prayer of thanks to God?

After all of the so-called wise men of Babylon sought answers, it was Daniel, a prisoner of war, who finally was able to save the day with an accurate description and interpretation. I wonder if it was tempting for Daniel to take the credit when he went before the king. He could have earned even more points in the king's eyes by pridefully acting as if he had a magical power superior to the other advisors. But Daniel remained humble.

Read Daniel 2:26-28 in the margin. How did Daniel show humility and give glory to God when he went before the king?

Daniel acknowledged that no human being could reveal the king's dream and then said, "But there is a God in heaven who reveals secrets" (Daniel 2:28). After Daniel humbly pointed to God, giving Him the credit, and told the king his dream and its meaning, King Nebuchadnezzar made a bold proclamation.

Read Daniel 2:47 in the margin. What did the king declare? How was Daniel's humility integral to the king's realization?

The king said to Daniel, "Truly, your God is the greatest of gods, the Lord over kings, a revealer of mysteries, for you have been able to reveal this secret."
(Daniel 2:47)

Just as Daniel's discipline saved him from dishonoring God in chapter 1, here in chapter 2 we see that his humility (plus a little wisdom and courage) not only saved his life and the lives of many others but also pointed the king of a pagan nation to the God of Israel. In Daniel 2:47 it's King Nebuchadnezzar who proclaims, "Your God is the greatest of gods, the Lord over kings."

Daniel is a good example of a humble spirit before God and others; but when it comes to humility, Jesus is the best example.

Read Philippians 2:3-5 in the margin. According to these verses, what does it mean to show the humility of Christ?

³Don't be selfish; don't try to impress others. Be humble, thinking of others as better than yourselves. ⁴Don't look out only for your own interests, but take an interest in others, too.

⁵You must have the same attitude [character] that Christ Jesus had.
(Philippians 2:3-5, author's addition)

How can you give more honor to others than to yourself today?

What adjustments do you need to make in order to have the same attitude or character of Christ?

What are some ways that our humility can point others to Christ?

Ultimately, the goal for every believer is to live into these verses from Philippians 2, adopting the same attitude or character as Christ. By coming from heaven to earth and giving His life for ours, Jesus showed perfect love and humility. Spend time with Him today, and allow His character to become your own.

Prayer

- Pick up a mirror, figuratively speaking. What do you see when you consider your current character traits?
- Jot down the character traits that you want to be evident in your life.
- Ask God to help you develop His character, leaving behind any attitudes or habits that do not reflect Jesus.

DAY 3: LIVING WITH INTEGRITY

Settle

Set a timer for two minutes and just be still. During those 120 seconds, allow your breathing and heart rate to slow as you escape the day's demands and quiet yourself before the Lord, giving Him your full attention.

Focus

Do not be conformed to this world, but be transformed by the renewing of your minds, so that you may discern what is the will of God—what is good and acceptable and perfect.

(Romans 12:2 NRSV)

[16]Shadrach, Meshach, and Abednego replied, "O Nebuchadnezzar, we do not need to defend ourselves before you. [17]If we are thrown into the blazing furnace, the God whom we serve is able to save us. He will rescue us from your power, Your Majesty. [18]But even if he doesn't, . . . we will never serve your gods."

(Daniel 3:16-18)

Reading Daniel's Story (optional): Read Daniel 7–9.

Reflect

My friend and long-time partner in ministry, Michael, is a Maasai tribesman from Kenya. He has done tremendous work for the people of Africa through building water wells, caring for orphans, planting churches, and sharing Christ. When Jim and I first met Michael, we asked him about his family. He shared that he had nine children—three biological and six adopted. He told us that when he invited these six children to become part of his family, he said, "I do not know that we can all live together. But I can promise you that you will not die alone. What I have I will share with you." Wow! What a great example of God's love.

Michael is one of my heroes!

While traveling with an American pastor in Northern Kenya recently, Michael's vehicle broke down in a particularly dangerous area. It became apparent that the two men would have to spend the night with the jeep and brave the predators of the area, both animal and human. As the sun set, the American pastor asked Michael, "Are we going to be okay?" to which Michael responded, "Yes, my brother! We will be okay—either way."

Either way! Perhaps this was not the response the pastor was looking for, but it shows what I have come to love so much about Michael. He has an eternal perspective of his earthly trials.

Our study this week is centered around the life of Daniel, a young man who, through no fault of his own, found himself living in a foreign country as a prisoner of war. Daniel and his friends encountered many messy situations while living in Babylon. They could have become depressed and discouraged as they faced one difficulty after another, but with God's help they found ways to thrive in their environment and maintain their values.

We've seen in chapters 1 and 2 that Daniel showed King Nebuchadnezzar how powerful the God of Israel is, but the king forgot these lessons and turned back to self-serving practices. In his encounters with Nebuchadnezzar in these two chapters, Daniel demonstrated not only discipline and humility but also integrity in the way he handled each delicate situation.

Today Daniel's friends take center stage in chapter 3, and we will see that not only Daniel displayed integrity but his faithful friends did as well. Just as bad company corrupts good character (1 Corinthians 15:33), good company promotes good character. This certainly seemed to have been true for Daniel and his friends.

Let me summarize the story. King Nebuchadnezzar had a giant golden statue of himself erected and then gave orders for the entire kingdom to bow down and worship his image at appointed times. Anyone who refused to obey his command would be thrown into a blazing-hot furnace. This presented a serious dilemma for Daniel's friends Shadrach, Meshach, and Abednego because they did not want to bow down to anyone or anything but the one true God.

Read Daniel 3:1-6, and describe the statue that King Nebuchadnezzar had built:

Who was to bow down and worship the statue? What would be the signal for them to do this, and what would happen to those who refused?

King Nebuchadnezzar's image of himself was made out of gold and stood sixty cubits high and six cubits wide—about ninety feet high and nine feet wide.[2] People of every race, nation, and language were to bow before the statue whenever they heard the music of the horn, flute, zither, lyre, harp, pipes, and other instruments. Those who refused would be thrown into a blazing furnace!

Shadrach, Meshach, and Abednego found themselves in a mess. They had a decision to make. Would they show integrity by honoring God and refusing to obey the order, risking their lives? Or would they conform to the standards of Babylonian culture and bow to this golden image? These faithful men had to answer these questions of integrity and conviction.

We face similar struggles today. We may not be required to bow before a golden statue, but we must answer similar questions of integrity and conviction. We must continually choose whether to conform to the expectations of society or stand for God's principles. Romans 12:2 gives us clear instructions for when we face these situations.

Reread Romans 12:2 (page 183). In what situations have you found yourself pressured to conform?

Is there a particular law or a rule that you find difficult to follow for reasons of integrity? If so, what is it, and what has been your response?

Daniel's friends were called out by name as not having complied with the order to worship the statue. The pressure to conform must have been tough for them. But they chose to remain faithful to God. This is a dilemma that we often face as well. There are times when our culture dictates behaviors that are contradictory to biblical standards. For instance, the use of profanity, sex outside of marriage, and greed are commonplace in our culture. But clearly these are in conflict with the godly standards we find in Scripture.

When culture conflicts with character, we have the opportunity to live with integrity.

When culture conflicts with character, we have the opportunity to live with integrity.

When Nebuchadnezzar heard that Shadrach, Meshach, and Abednego would not bow to his image, he was enraged. In fact, he ordered them to be burned alive. Of course, this was not what these men had hoped for, but they faced their sentence with faith and courage.

Reread Daniel 3:16-18 (page 183). How did they respond to the king? What did they say about their God?

Talk about not conforming! Shadrach, Meshach, and Abednego did not yield their principles but stood for God even in the face of death. They knew that God had the power to save them from the fire; but even if He didn't, they would not succumb to this earthly king's power and worship the statue. Like my friend Michael, they knew that they would be okay either way. By living with an eternal perspective and unshakable values, they were able to maintain their integrity.

The king was furious at their refusal to worship the statue and had the three men thrown into the fiery furnace. But God was with them through their persecution. The men were bound and thrown into a furnace that had been heated to seven times its usual heat. In fact, the guards who threw them into the fire were killed as the flames leapt from the furnace. But we see that God's faithful men of integrity were spared this torture:

[24]But suddenly, Nebuchadnezzar jumped up in amazement and exclaimed to his advisers, "Didn't we tie up three men and throw them into the furnace?"

"Yes, Your Majesty, we certainly did," they replied.

[25]"Look!" Nebuchadnezzar shouted. "I see four men, unbound, walking around in the fire unharmed! And the fourth looks like a god!"

[26]Then Nebuchadnezzar came as close as he could to the door of the flaming furnace and shouted: "Shadrach, Meshach, and Abednego, servants of the Most High God, come out! Come here!"

So Shadrach, Meshach, and Abednego stepped out of the fire. [27]Then the high officers, officials, governors, and advisers crowded around them and saw that *the fire had not touched them. Not a hair on their heads was singed, and their clothing was not scorched. They didn't even smell of smoke!*

²⁸*Then Nebuchadnezzar said, "Praise to the God of Shadrach, Meshach, and Abednego! He sent his angel to rescue his servants who trusted in him. They defied the king's command and were willing to die rather than serve or worship any god except their own God.*

²⁹*. . . There is no other god who can rescue like this!"*

(Daniel 3:24-29)

I love that the text gives us the detail that not even their clothes smelled of smoke! Their integrity and courage in the face of conflict led to a miraculous deliverance that brought the king to a tremendous conclusion.

What was the king's response to God's rescue of Shadrach, Meshach, and Abednego?

Nebuchadnezzar witnessed God's power at work in a miraculous way, and it led him to a new understanding and respect of the God of Daniel and his friends. Integrity in the face of opposition speaks loudly to others.

What about our own lives? Will we be protected from every fiery trial? The simple answer is no. This is a broken planet, and sometimes life simply is not fair. And as we face our own fiery furnaces, we will have the opportunity to stand or to fold. Like Shadrach, Meshach, and Abednego, may we have the strength to stand even when the outcome is unclear. Because in those painful moments, we can know with confidence that God will be with us.

Read Isaiah 43:2 in the margin. What is God's promise to us?

What's heating up in your life? Are you facing anxiety or depression, sickness, marital strife, custody battles, or loneliness? Perhaps you're simply overwhelmed with life in general. Whatever "fire" you are facing today, God wants you to invite Him to walk with you so that you don't have to go through it alone.

> **Integrity in the face of opposition speaks loudly to others.**

> *When you go through deep waters,*
> *I will be with you.*
> *When you go through rivers of difficulty,*
> *you will not drown.*
> *When you walk through the fire of oppression,*
> *you will not be burned up;*
> *the flames will not consume you.*
> (Isaiah 43:2)

*7b[God] is a
shield to those
who walk with
integrity.
8He guards the
paths of the just
and protects
those who are
faithful to him.
(Proverbs 2:7b-8)*

Read Proverbs 2:7b-8 in the margin. How can these verses bring you comfort in your current situation?

God is a shield to those who walk with integrity. Isn't that a great promise? God guards and protects those who are faithful to Him. That's incredible!

Don't be discouraged when you face fiery trials. Remember that you are not alone. You serve a God who walks with His faithful ones in the fire. His angels stand guard. And in the long run—for all of eternity—not a hair on your head will be singed!

Pray

- Listen to "Even If," recorded by MercyMe.
- Take time to pray for those who are persecuted around the world. You may want to check out www.persecution.com for ways you can get involved.
- Claim the promise of Isaiah 43:2 and ask God to walk with you as you navigate the deep waters and walk through the fire you are facing in your life.

DAY 4: CHOOSING A LIFE OF WISDOM

Settle

Tune out the troubles of the day with a favorite song and allow the words to bring peace to your heart.

Focus

⁶For the Lᴏʀᴅ gives wisdom;
  from his mouth come knowledge and understanding;
⁷he stores up sound wisdom for the upright.

(Proverbs 2:6-7a ESV)

[The queen mother said,] ¹²"This man Daniel ... has exceptional ability and is filled with divine knowledge and understanding. He can interpret dreams, explain riddles, and solve difficult problems. Call for Daniel, and he will tell you what the writing means." ... [King Belshazzar said to Daniel,] ¹⁴"I have heard ... that you are filled with insight, understanding, and wisdom."

(Daniel 5:12, 14)

If any of you lacks wisdom, you should ask God, who gives generously to all without finding fault, and it will be given to you.

(James 1:5 NIV)

Reading Daniel's Story (optional): Read Daniel 10–12.

Reflect

I was having a delightful lunch with my daughter and everything was great until her food arrived and she said in exasperation, "I'm just like Belshazzar! I never learn from my mistakes."

"What? Belshazzar, like the guy in the Book of Daniel?" I asked.

"Yes! I know I don't like the macaroni and cheese here, yet I order it again and again. What is wrong with me? When will I learn?"

It was an odd reference, but one I'm not likely to forget! Today as we look again into the life of Daniel, we will see that King Belshazzar, King Nebuchadnezzar's grandson, did not learn from previous mistakes; and it cost him his reign, his life, and the kingdom. Daniel, on the other hand, once again handled a delicate situation well, demonstrating another valuable character trait: wisdom.

According to Proverbs 2:6-7a (page 189), what is the source of wisdom?

Do yourself a favor and learn all you can; then remember what you learn and you will prosper.
(Proverbs 19:8 GNT)

Read Proverbs 19:8 in the margin. What are we to do with wisdom, and why?

Recall a time when you relied on God's wisdom (Scripture) as opposed to your own plan? How did it work out?

Recall a time when you ignored God's wisdom (Scripture) and pursued your plan, knowing it was in opposition to God's. How did that work out?

I hope that you've been taking time this week to read through the Book of Daniel. His life is a series of trials. As a teenager, Daniel faced a major crisis when he was taken as a prisoner of war into a foreign land. He made the bold choice not to conform to the standards of this new pagan country, and he wisely and creatively found ways to maintain the values of his faith. By staying close to God, Daniel was able not only to survive but also to thrive in a hostile environment.

In chapter 5, we see that Daniel was no longer a teenager. He had served the king faithfully for decades, eventually leading Nebuchadnezzar to praise the God of Israel. When Nebuchadnezzar died, the king was succeeded by his grandson, Belshazzar. No doubt Belshazzar's mother and grandfather

had shared with him the lessons learned by watching Daniel's life. Perhaps they even had pointed him toward the God of Israel, but Belshazzar was not interested. He was living according to his own plans. As we read in Proverbs, "There is a way that appears to be right, / but in the end it leads to death" (14:12 NIV).

When Belshazzar had been king for only two years, he threw a party for a thousand of his friends while the enemy encamped around Babylon. He and his friends got drunk and misused the sacred goblets from Jerusalem's temple to toast to pagan gods. (Really bad idea, by the way.) Then the hand of God suddenly appeared and miraculously wrote a mysterious message on the wall of the palace.

Read Daniel 5:5-9, and summarize below what happened after the writing appeared on the wall:

Now reread Daniel 5:12, 14 (page 189). Why did the queen mother suggest the king summon Daniel?

When no one could read what had been written, the queen mother suggested that Daniel be summoned. She reminded Belshazzar of the wisdom Daniel had brought to the kingdom under Nebuchadnezzar's reign. In Daniel 5:11 we read, "There is a man in your kingdom who has within him the spirit of the holy gods. During Nebuchadnezzar's reign, this man was found to have insight, understanding, and wisdom." So again Daniel was called upon for wisdom.

Belshazzar promised to make Daniel a very rich and powerful man if he would reveal the mystery of the writing on the wall. But Daniel wanted no reward for listening to God. His years of service to God had brought him the maturity, wisdom, and security that came from knowing that God was with him.

In Daniel 5:25-30, the message from the writing on the wall is revealed. Daniel explained to King Belshazzar that his reign was coming to an abrupt

Wisdom is seeing things from God's perspective and responding in ways that please Him.

end. Babylon had been judged and condemned for their pagan practices and idol worship. In fact, Belshazzar was killed that very night, and the kingdom was stripped from the Babylonians. Belshazzar lacked wisdom.

Wisdom is seeing things from God's perspective and responding in ways that please Him. But just knowing what we should do is not enough. We have to put it into action. Daniel did both, even when it was scary.

Wisdom is truth lived out, which spares us from pain and brings us blessings.

Read James 3:13-17. What are the benefits of living wisely?

How have you seen people search for truth in ways other than turning to God?

I don't know many people who would say that they don't want wisdom. Many of us like the idea of living by God's truths—until we find a truth that we don't like. It happens all the time. We want God's blessings, but we don't want to live according to all of God's standards. Some of the most common areas where people choose their desire over God's wisdom, for example, have to do with sexual relationships and money. So many people want God to bless their relationships. They truly desire God's best in their finances. But they do not live according to His standards in these areas; and as a result, they live from one mess to another. This is not wise.

Wisdom is looking beyond our own perspective to see things from God's viewpoint—and then choosing to live from that wisdom. This can be difficult because our perspective is what we tend to know best; and doing what we want, even if it's not the best decision, tends to be what we do.

The Bible tells us that King Solomon was the wisest man who ever lived. He wrote a great deal on the subject of wisdom, such as:

Getting wisdom is the wisest thing you can do!
(Proverbs 4:7a)

For wisdom is far more valuable than rubies.
Nothing you desire can compare with it.
(Proverbs 8:11)

The fear of the LORD *is the beginning of knowledge,*
    but fools despise wisdom and instruction.
                          (Proverbs 1:7 NIV)

Is it possible to live according to God's Word and yet be disobedient to its truths? Explain your response.

In what areas and/or situations do you need to abandon your view and embrace God's wisdom?

Daniel truly lived a remarkable life of wisdom, but I wonder if he would see it that way. (I hope to ask him when we meet in heaven.) He might say, "It wasn't remarkable at all." He may see himself as just an ordinary guy who chose to be faithful and rely on God's wisdom during tough times. But friend, that is what being remarkable is all about—relying on God's wisdom no matter what mess we face.

Choose to be remarkable and wise!

Pray

- Make James 1:5 (NIV) your prayer today: "If any of you lacks wisdom, you should ask God, who gives generously to all without finding fault, and it will be given to you."
- Ask God for new insights into your current situation and the courage to live according to His plan, not your own.
- Thank God that His wisdom, blessings, and goodness are available to you today.

DAY 5: HAVING COURAGE

Settle

As you begin your time with God today, listen to "Reckless Love," recorded by Cory Asbury, and be encouraged. God is with you, and you can be an overcomer no matter what mess life throws your way!

Focus

Having courage in the midst of our personal storms will help us weather them well.

*"Be strong and courageous. Do not be afraid or terrified . . . for the L*ORD* your God goes with you; he will never leave you nor forsake you."*

(Deuteronomy 31:6 NIV)

When Daniel learned that the law had been signed, he went home and knelt down as usual in his upstairs room, with its windows open toward Jerusalem.

(Daniel 6:10)

Reflect

Welcome to the final day of our Messy People journey! I hope that you have had some precious times with Jesus over these six weeks and that He has spoken new truths of peace and joy into your life. As we end our study today, I want to lead you to focus on a fifth characteristic we see in Daniel's life: courage.

Through our time together I've shared with you several of my favorite verses. John 16:33, however, is not one of them! In this verse Jesus says, "I've told you all this so that trusting me, you will be unshakable and assured, deeply at peace. In this godless world you will continue to experience difficulties. But take heart! I've conquered the world" (John 16:33 MSG). This verse tells us the truth, but I wish all of it didn't have to be our truth! I wish it said, "In this world you may experience difficulties!" But it doesn't. God tells us in advance: there will be struggles. Problems are going to come our way. Our lives will be messy at times. It's a given. That's the part of the verse I'm not so crazy about. But the promise it contains is powerful: "But take heart! I've conquered the world." And when we believe this and trust Jesus, we will be unshakable and at peace!

Isn't that precious of God? He gives us a heads-up that problems are part of the human condition, but He also promises us that by trusting in

Him we can face these struggles and even have peace in the midst of them. Having courage in the midst of our personal storms will help us weather them well.

Over the years I've had the opportunity to teach many kids how to swim. The ones who caught on quickly had two things in common: courage and trust. Courage to put their little faces in the water and kick, kick, kick; and trust to know that I would not let anything bad happen to them through the process. Eventually, they all learned. With some of the kids, it was a really fun process for us both. But with others, it was awful for us both! The difference came down to trust and courage.

Our lives are messy. Sometimes messes come through our own choices, as with the prodigal son. Or perhaps like Josiah, we are born into a family that comes with a lot of mess. Or maybe the mess we are facing is more like what David faced against his critics. Whatever the case, Scripture has already told us that this should not surprise us; in fact, as we will soon see, we actually should expect difficulties in life. The key is to handle these difficulties in ways that honor Christ, just as Daniel did.

Perhaps Daniel's most famous trial came when he was an elderly man. Daniel had distinguished himself through discipline, humility, integrity, and wisdom the entire time he was held captive in Babylon. Even while living as an exile, God's favor and Daniel's character brought him to a position of honor in a foreign land. Not only did he thrive under the rule of Nebuchadnezzar and his grandson, Belshazzar; his service made him stand out to the new king, Darius.

In chapter 6 we read that Daniel had risen to become one of the three most influential leaders in the kingdom. His success did not go unnoticed or without some jealousy on the part of other leaders around him. So they began to plot a way to tear him down.

The other administrators and officials searched for some fault in the way Daniel was handling his affairs, but they couldn't find anything to criticize. He was faithful and honest and always responsible. They concluded, "Our only chance of finding grounds for accusing Daniel will be in connection with the rules of his religion" (Daniel 6:5). So the administrators and high officers went to the king with a well-prepared speech:

> ⁶"Long live King Darius! ⁷We are all in agreement . . . that the king should make a law that will be strictly enforced. Give orders that for the next thirty days any person who prays to anyone, divine or human—except to you, Your Majesty—

will be thrown into the den of lions. ⁸And now, Your Majesty, issue and sign this law so it cannot be changed, an official law of the Medes and Persians that cannot be revoked."

(Daniel 6:6-8)

We're told in the next verse that King Darius signed the law. But rather than react in fear when he learned that the law had been signed, Daniel went home and followed his usual routine.

Read Daniel 6:10. What did Daniel do?

Daniel knelt down as usual in his upstairs room, with its windows open toward Jerusalem. This is important to note. Even though the penalty of praying to anyone other than the king was death in a pit of lions, Daniel did not waver in his practices of honoring God. In fact, he did not even attempt to hide his prayers, choosing to pray in his upstairs room with the windows open. Daniel courageously and faithfully maintained his values.

If I were in Daniel's situation, I'd like to think I too would have been faithful and continued as usual to pray. But if I'm honest, I probably would have shut those windows and closed the blinds. It can be difficult to boldly practice our faith in the face of trials and challenges and persecution.

Has there been a time when you found it difficult to boldly practice your faith in the face of trials, challenges, or persecution for your beliefs or practices as a Christian? If so, describe it briefly:

When I became a follower of Christ, I expected life to become easier, and in some ways it did. It was easier in that I was not alone. It was comforting to know that the struggles and pains of this world would no longer be with me in heaven. But as far as all my problems going away—well, that just didn't happen. The mean kids at school were still mean to me. The acne was still on my face. Is this how it works? I wondered. I learned that yes, it is actually.

Read 1 Peter 4:12 in the margin. How would you restate this verse in your own words?

Dear friends, don't be surprised at the fiery trials you are going through, as if something strange were happening to you.
(1 Peter 4:12)

Sometimes life is messy, and at times the messes feel completely overwhelming. God does not promise to spare us difficulties, but He does promise to be with us through them. And that is enough! What is required of us in those messy situations is to be courageous and hold fast to our faith. Like the children in my swim classes through the years, we must trust God and have courage.

Recall the situation you described previously. What helped you to have courage during this time? What happened?

> **God does not promise to spare us difficulties, but He does promise to be with us through them.**

In Daniel's situation, the plot to have him arrested succeeded. But the plot to destroy him never stood a chance!

> [19]At the first light of dawn, the king got up and hurried to the lions' den. [20]When he came near the den, he called to Daniel in an anguished voice, "Daniel, servant of the living God, has your God, whom you serve continually, been able to rescue you from the lions?"
>
> [21]Daniel answered, "May the king live forever! [22]My God sent his angel, and he shut the mouths of the lions. They have not hurt me, because I was found innocent in his sight. Nor have I ever done any wrong before you, Your Majesty."
>
> [23]The king was overjoyed and gave orders to lift Daniel out of the den. And when Daniel was lifted from the den, no wound was found on him, because he had trusted in his God.
>
> (Daniel 6:19-23 NIV)

How did God rescue Daniel, and what was the king's response?

If Daniel's story ended here, it would be great. He was saved from a torturous death in the lion's den. But there's more!

25Then King Darius sent this message to the people of every race and nation and language throughout the world:

"Peace and prosperity to you!

26"I decree that everyone throughout my kingdom should tremble with fear before the God of Daniel.

For he is the living God,
and he will endure forever.

His kingdom will never be destroyed,
and his rule will never end.

27He rescues and saves his people;
he performs miraculous signs and wonders
in the heavens and on earth.

He has rescued Daniel
from the power of the lions."

28So Daniel prospered during the reign of Darius and the reign of Cyrus the Persian.

(Daniel 6:25-28)

When King Darius observed the faith of Daniel and the power of his God, he proclaimed that the entire kingdom should honor and worship God!

How might this story have been different if Daniel had been too afraid to continue his prayer habit?

How might your faith and courage impact those around you?

According to Matthew 10:32-33 (in the margin), what is the guarantee for everyone who publicly acknowledges and honors God here on earth?

Daniel was able to stand strong because he knelt often. Daniel's practice of honoring God in his life gave him the courage to face whatever came his way; and in so doing, he proved to be a testimony to others, including the king. Throughout his life, Daniel lived with an eternal perspective despite his temporary difficulties. This is an advanced maneuver but one that will serve us all well as we face the challenges of our own lives.

As our study comes to a close, I hope you're more convinced than ever that God chooses to use and transform broken people and messy situations. We've seen how He did it with Rahab, the prodigal son, Josiah, Mary, David, and Daniel, and He will do it for us, too. If you'll give God your mess, He will turn it into a masterpiece!

Pray

- Thank God for Who He is and for His everlasting love toward you!
- As you pray, receive God's love, letting it invade and fill your heart so that you may carry it with you as you live your best life.
- Ask for the courage to live boldly into the calling God has for your life.
- Surrender your mess to God, and invite Him to turn it into a masterpiece!

32"Everyone who acknowledges me publicly here on earth, I will also acknowledge before my Father in heaven. 33But everyone who denies me here on earth, I will also deny before my Father in heaven."
(Matthew 10:32-33)

If you'll give God your mess, He will turn it into a masterpiece!

"Dear friends, your real home is not here on earth. You are strangers here. I ask you to keep away from all the sinful desires of the flesh. These things fight to get hold of your soul."

(1 Peter 2:11 NLV)

"My prayer is not that you take them out of the world but that you protect them from the evil one. They are not of the world, even as I am not of it. Sanctify them by the truth; your word is truth. As you sent me into the world, I have sent them into the world."

(John 17:15-18 NIV)

Jesus is praying that we, His followers, would be _____ but not isolated while on earth.

As Jesus people, we need to first allow God to clean up our own messes and honor God like Daniel did through faithfulness and boldness, and then we need to _____ _____ in tough places.

"I have told you these things, so that in me you may have peace. In this world you will have trouble. But take heart! I have overcome the world."

(John 16:33 NIV)

In Christ we can have peace . . . if we go ahead and decide that we'll handle the messes of our lives with _____ and _____.

VIDEO VIEWER GUIDE: ANSWERS

Week 1

need

centered

godly people

future

Week 2

first move

stuff

carefully

kindly

reconciliation / resolution

Week 3

procrastinate

victim

temptation

control

Week 4

decide / respond

courage / new ways

changed / partner

Week 5

carefully

cool

information

what you can

Pray

Week 6

insulated

show up

faith / holiness

Notes

Week 1

1. Kaushik, "11 Oldest Continuously Inhabited Cities in the World," *Amusing Planet*, July 2, 2012, http://www.amusingplanet.com/2012/07/11-continuously-inhabited -oldest-cities.html. Accessed June 19, 2018.

Week 2

1. "The 'Kezazah Ceremony,'" Creative Kidswork, https://www.creativekidswork.com /all-ideas/142-101-the-kezazah-ceremony-sunday-school-children-ministry-ideas. Accessed June 20, 2018.
2. Bart Jansen, "Nearly 56,000 Bridges Called Structurally Deficient," USA *Today*, February 15, 2017, https://www.usatoday.com/story/news/2017/02/15/deficient -bridges/97890324/. Accessed June 21, 2018.

Week 4

1. "Trust and Obey," words by John H. Sammis, 1887, in *The United Methodist Hymnal* (Nashville: The United Methodist Publishing House, 1989), 467.
2. "John Wayne Legacy Quotes," John Wayne Enterprises website, https://johnwayne .com/quotes/. Accessed June 15, 2018.

Week 5

1. "The Man, the Boy, and the Donkey," AesopFables.com, http://aesopfables.com/cgi /aesop1.cgi?3&TheMantheBoyandtheDonkey. Accessed June 25, 2018.
2. Tim Stevens and Tony Morgan, *Simply Strategic Stuff: Help for Leaders Drowning in the Details of Running a Church* (Loveland, CO: Group Publishing, Inc.), 28–29.

Week 6

1. "The Destruction of the Southern Kingdom of Judah: Fall of Jerusalem," Bible History Online website, https://www.bible-history.com/map_fall_of_judah /fallofjudah_fall_of_jerusalem.html. Accessed June 24, 2018.
2. Contributed by www.walvoord.com (John F. Walvoord website), "3. The Golden Image of Nebuchadnezzar," Bible.org, https://bible.org/seriespage/3-golden-image -nebuchadnezzar. Accessed June 24, 2018.

More Women's Bible Studies From Abingdon Women
Your Life. Your Faith.

Numbers: Learning Contentment in a Culture of More
Say no to the desire for bigger, better, faster, and more.

Workbook ISBN:
9781501801747

First Corinthians: Living Love When We Disagree
Show love when you disagree without compromising your convictions.

Workbook ISBN:
9781501801686

Elijah: Spiritual Stamina in Every Season
Go the distance in the life of faith.

Available August 2018

Workbook ISBN:
9781501838910

Joseph: The Journey to Forgiveness
Find freedom through forgiveness.

Workbook ISBN:
9781426789106

Jeremiah: Daring to Hope in an Unstable World
Learn to surrender to God's will and rest your hope in Him alone.

Workbook ISBN:
9781426788871

A Woman Overwhelmed: A Bible Study on the Life of Mary, the Mother of Jesus
Go from overwhelmed by life to overwhelmed by God.

Workbook ISBN:
9781501839924

Joshua: Winning the Worry Battle
Be victorious over worry in your life!

Workbook ISBN:
9781501813603

Never Alone: 6 Encounters with Jesus to Heal Your Deepest Hurts
Journey with six hurting women in the Gospels to experience the healing power of Jesus' unconditional love.

Workbook ISBN:
9781501845826

Becoming Heart Sisters: A Bible Study on Authentic Friendships
Explore the Bible and learn to cultivate God-honoring relationships.

Workbook ISBN:
9781501821202

Beautiful Already: Reclaiming God's Perspective on Beauty
See yourself as God sees you.

Workbook ISBN:
9781501813542

She Dreams: Live the Life You Were Created For
Discover and follow your God-given dreams by looking to the biblical story of Moses.

Coming Feb. 2019

Study Guide ISBN:
9781501878343
Book ISBN:
9781501878329

Determined: Living Like Jesus in Every Moment
Learn to live each day to the fullest and make a difference for God's kingdom through a study of Jesus' choices in the Gospel of Luke.

Workbook ISBN:
9781501878862

Coming Apr. 2019

DVD, leader guide, and kit also available for each Bible study.
Find samples at AbingdonWomen.com

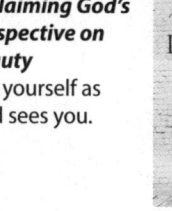

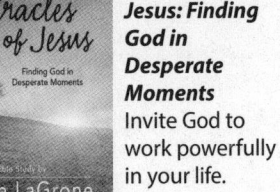
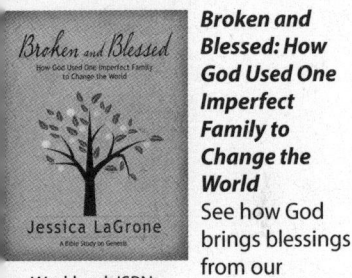

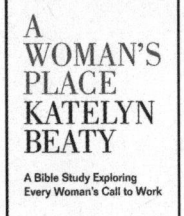